DATE DUE

Demco, Inc. 38-293

Protestantism and the American University

◆

William Warren Sweet (1881-1959)

Protestantism and the American University

An Intellectual Biography of
WILLIAM WARREN SWEET

James L. Ash, Jr.

Foreword by MARTIN E. MARTY

SMU PRESS • DALLAS

Library of Congress Cataloging in Publication Data

Ash, James L., 1945-
    Protestantism and the American university.

    Bibliography: p.
    Includes index.
    1. Sweet, William Warren, 1881-1959. 2. Church
historians—United States—Biography. I. Title.
BR139.S93A83   1982   277.3′0092′4 [B]   82-10629
ISBN 0-87074-183-7

Contents

Foreword

A FOREWORD allows its author to show regard for and to locate the importance of the writer and the subject of a book. Professor Ash would be embarrassed if I dwelt on him, but I know he will welcome a show of regard and even affection for his subject, historian William Warren Sweet.

A foreword allows its author to be a bit personal, to draw the curtain back in an almost folksy manner before the serious author sets the characters on stage for a sober drama. In that personal mood, I can perhaps best introduce Sweet.

As Ash shows, back in the 1920s Professor Sweet became the first established American university professor freed to devote his career to the study of American religious history. History as a subject came rather late to the modern academy. Americans made best sellers of historical works in the nineteenth century, but most of these were by clerics, lawyers, and other gentlepersons. Not until nearly the end of the century did a cohort of professional historians, adopting European seminar models, bring "science" to their art—sometimes at the loss of art.

Americans were religious and were curious about religion, but few historians took up the religious theme. They were busy writing about politics, patriotism, or the emergence of industrial America. Some of them had repudiated the small-town religion of their childhood and found the subject to be ignorable and dismissible. William Warren Sweet, however, schooled himself in the best ways to go about writing history in his time and brought a lifelong interest in religion to his vocation. He fused the two. The University of Chicago, liking what it saw, invited him to a chair in American church history. During the next nearly two decades, Sweet busied himself getting out of the chair to gather documents, chiefly on religion on the frontier, and then getting back to it to edit and write volume upon volume.

Now for the personal note: Sweet is my "spiritual grandfather"; he trained Sidney E. Mead, who succeeded him; Mead trained me and I succeeded him. So much for the begats. I am by coincidence typing this on the last day of my nineteenth year in the post, which is exactly how long Sweet held it. To read on these pages what he accomplished in those years is humbling indeed.

Rather than use it as an exercise in humility on one hand or a kind of name-dropping on the other, I want to use the personal tie to locate this book and its different world. Sweet looked out on classes made up entirely of Protestants, presumably almost all of them white, male, and of mainline church traditions.

As he looked out on a homogeneous WASP group, he could also, as Ash shows, look back on a world where Methodist, Protestant, and Christian values shaped the universe of shopkeepers, homemakers, teachers, and little boys, in Baldwin, Kansas. As this book shows, in many ways Sweet "never left home," and never had the problem of "you can't go home again." He carried that home with him to Chicago and later to Dallas, or wherever he followed his craft and vocation.

That spiritual or psychic home provided him with what philosopher George Santayana called a *locus standi*, a place to view the world, a universe of meanings and a provider of dimensions. Its coziness bred a kind of a cocoon around him, one that screened out, for example, Catholics. When they showed up they looked the way anything must that becomes visible in a cocoon: as ominous, dark, and threatening. Similarly, Sweet paid little attention to Jews, who weren't quite a part of "church history" and who had done little on the frontier. Blacks were people for whom abolitionists had done something, but they were hardly agents of their own history. While Sweet developed competence in Latin American history, he did not develop commensurate love for Latin people.

Today, on my last day in a comparable nineteen-year span, but long, I hope, before I give my "Every Dog Has His Day and I've Had Mine" speech (see Ash's story of Sweet's speech at retirement), I look out on a different world. While I came from a Nebraska town much like his Kansas one, the classroom provided a very different perspective. When I began teaching in 1963 Vatican II was in process. Just about then Roman Catholics started to arrive in numbers in my part of the country, but I could still look back on Sweet's world in the classroom.

Today's class was not large. There were, by happenstance, no blacks in it, but the black narrative looms large in today's story of American religious history. There were Jews, uneasy with the concept of "church history," but eager to trace their part in the American plot. Three Orientals reminded us that there was American immigration from the West, as well as from the East. A healthy minority of the class were women, who will not permit the story to be told as Sweet told it—almost macho style, with a tinge of frontier swagger. As for the rest, there were more people with Italian, Irish, or German than with WASP names. There were more Catholics than Protestants, more people from conservative than from mainline Protestant backgrounds. And our graduate school is still a somewhat domesticated sample of American pluralism. Professor Ash, looking up from his classes at the University of Miami with its richer, almost wild pluralism, would smile a bit benignly at my rather homogeneous, "half-way-back-to-Sweet" universe.

Telling the story today, therefore, means accounting for the sufferings and triumphs of all these people whose ancestors were at the margins of Sweet's plots, stories that Ash well outlines in the pages that follow. The narrative today has become far more complex and subtle. Yet it makes no sense without its backdrop. What was the canon, the set of codes, by which historians determined what was important or who belonged in the story? Ash uses Sweet to help answer such questions. He does so without condescension or without being patronizing. His smiles are at best knowing half-smiles, mere twinkles, and they do not come with sneers. He knows that in another nineteen years his universe and mine are likely to look remote, cozy, arcane. If he judges Sweet, he tends to do so in the context of the possibilities of Sweet's own time. That is how it should be in history.

The Sweet canon summarized a century of defining. It may be that less has changed than one might think as she or he reads of Baldwin, Kansas, and the man who never left home. To this day, only one of the numerous general histories of American religion has been written by a woman, only one by a non-Protestant. They both happen to be the same person, Catherine Albanese. Otherwise, Jews still write of the Jewish past, Catholics of the Catholic lore, and Protestants or ex-Protestants of the larger story, inevitably with a Protestant bias. I hope that Ash's location of Sweet and his definition of the code will stimulate a new generation to look for still other angles on the story.

Ash does not write about Sweet only to show how earnest he was, or how narrow were the limits he unwittingly set about his busyness and business, or how much we've advanced beyond Sweet. He recognizes the achievement of a master of his own sort, and pays due respects. William Warren Sweet is not and does not bid fair to become a household word. America is too divided into specialties and disciplines for that to happen. But Ash, by pointing to his distinctiveness, does a service in one more respect. I can point to that best by showing how Sweet stood out from other social scientists and planners in his day.

Jean Quandt in *From the Small Town to the Great Community* has shown how turn-of-the-century progressive intellectuals, most of them born in the Baldwin, Kansases of America, moved from them to the great city. John Dewey, Jane Addams, Josiah Royce, Charles Horton Cooley, and others took models from their ordered small town worlds and tried to use them in the great and disordered cities. To a person, however, they formally left behind the religion of their childhood. Along the way, they tended to undervalue or dismiss the role of religion in human affairs and gave a distorted picture of the common life of the people. Sweet left the small town physically, but, unlike the others, he did not reject the memory or potential of church and religious life. Isolating such a figure helps fill in the blanks on what better-known people of his day missed as they defined and prescribed for America.

Let William Warren Sweet have his moment, then. It is not likely that he will be given prominence beyond what he deserves. But he will be given attention for the way he serves a new generation in its own tasks of definition and prescription. For making him available, we are in debt to James Ash.

MARTIN E. MARTY

University of Chicago
June, 1982

Introduction

IN THE FIRST HALF of the twentieth century, professors of history in American universities, influenced by the rapidly changing world around them, wrought a quiet revolution in the way they perceived America's past. The masterful nineteenth-century vision of Frederick Jackson Turner, who defined American culture in terms of its frontier origins, had dominated the field of American history for a generation. As historians turned their attention away from the Protestant, rural America of the frontier toward the urban, industrial society which dominated their own landscape, many found that Turner's explanations became less relevant to the historical problems with which they dealt. Historians of American religion, however, at first generally failed to participate in this revision of American history. As Timothy Smith pointed out as late as 1957, most historians of American religion continued to focus on Turner's frontier as determinative.[1] This emphasis was in no small part a credit to the influence of the chief founder of their professional discipline, William Warren Sweet (1881-1959).

Professor Sweet never discarded his frontier emphasis. Though he spent most of his career in Chicago, one of America's leading urban centers, he focused not on the cities but rather on the western frontier for his normative model of American religion. He lived on Chicago's South Side, near one of the largest black communities in the country, yet he devoted little more than a few disparaging remarks to the contributions of blacks to American religion. During Sweet's lifetime the largest single religious body in America was unquestionably the Roman Catholic church, yet he consistently and consciously ignored Roman Catholicism in favor of emphasizing several major Protestant bodies. While other historians were turning to the late nineteenth century to explain the complexities of their multiethnic, urban, industrial society, Sweet continued to point to an earlier era, the national period, as being especially important for the understanding of contemporary American religion.

Sweet's historical portrait of American religion defined the problem and set the terms for a generation of American religious historians, largely because of his extraordinarily successful career as an author and a teacher. In 1927, the Divinity School of the University of Chicago appointed him professor of the history of American Christianity, the first such position to be established by any university. During his forty-seven-year career he published some twenty-seven books and over fifty monographs on Methodism, the frontier, and American religion. As late as the 1960s American history textbooks routinely cited Sweet as the authoritative historian of American religion. Many of today's Protestant ministers were introduced to American religious history in seminary study through Sweet's major synthetic work, *The Story of Religions in America*, which appeared in three editions over its forty-three-year history at Harper & Row. Sweet directed more than thirty doctoral dissertations in American religious history. His students and their heirs still exercise a disproportionately large influence on their discipline.

Such was Sweet's influence that in his 1959 obituary the *Christian Century* called him the "father of American church history."[2] This term was technically inaccurate, for there had been dozens of American church historians since the time of William Bradford in the seventeenth century. Sweet was, however, the first trained, professional, American historian who specialized in religion, and as such did have the honor of establishing his field of study as a proper academic discipline free from ecclesiastical interests. Edwin S. Gaustad thus gives him a central place in his survey of American religious historiography:

The contributions of Sweet inaugurated American church history as a separate discipline, within the university as opposed to the seminary. And Sweet's own historiographical stance reveals the continuing evolution of that discipline, seeking its proper level in the academic market place.[3]

Other historians, notably William Clebsch,[4] Jerald Brauer,[5] Henry May,[6] and Sydney Ahlstrom,[7] trace a current renaissance in American religious studies back to Sweet's era. Given such a renaissance and Sweet's unquestioned position in it, it is essential that Sweet's own perspective on the development of American religion be understood.

Sweet himself consistently denied that he held any a priori assumptions concerning American religious life. He was unaware of the limiting effects of the decidedly Protestant, Anglo-Saxon prejudices which underlay his interpretations. He claimed to be completely objective, and in his day he won respect among secular historians by professing to abandon the "denominational propaganda" which had previously dominated much of American religious history.[8] His connection with the prolific "Chicago school" of historians of Christianity helped to establish his reputation as a "scientific" historian with, in his words, "no side to defend, no party to uphold."[9] When compared with the dozens of eulogistic denominational histories which his synthetic works were written to replace, Sweet's method and conclusions do seem objective, broader in scope, and refreshingly free of denominational polemics.

The idea of totally unbiased, "scientific" history, however, is an idea whose time has passed.[10] Today practically no credible academic figure would claim that history is a presentation of facts alone. Instead, it is widely recognized that the historian must select, organize, and interpret facts, that all historians view facts within the limitations of some philosophical perspective, and that totally unbiased history is indeed impossible in addition to being of perhaps questionable value.

Contemporary historians of American religion thus have not accepted Sweet's claim of total objectivity. They have pointed out that Sweet shared the perspective of most previous historical synthesizers of American religion.[11] Like Robert Baird (1843), Daniel Dorchester (1888), Leonard Bacon (1897), and Henry Rowe (1924), Sweet located the constitutive elements of American religion in an evangelical Protestant establishment. Like these historians, he showed the uniqueness of this establishment in comparison to European patterns and was preoccupied with the theme of institutional growth. Sweet's distinctive contribution to this traditional perspective was his careful attention to the development of frontier Methodism as the key to an understanding of the Protestant establishment, and therefore to the whole of American religion.

Previous works on Sweet[12] provide at best, however, a limited criticism of his thought. Their consistent tendency is to treat Sweet's ideas in isolation from other aspects of his life. They leave unanswered the basic interpretive question, namely, how can we account for both what Sweet emphasized and what he ignored in his highly selective portrait of American religion? This work suggests that a key which will enable us to understand Sweet's perspective is the relationship of his ideas to the biographical setting in which they developed. The representativeness of such a biographical setting expands the relevance of the work, and helps to illustrate and explain the extraordinary tenacity of Protestant social ideas in the increasing secularity of the developing twentieth-century American university.

JAMES L. ASH, JR.

University of Miami
Coral Gables, Florida

Protestantism and the American University

---◆---

1

The Context of Childhood

ON A HOT AUGUST AFTERNOON in 1872, William Henry Sweet, later
to become the father of William Warren Sweet, wandered alone on
the outskirts of Piper City, Illinois, pondering the future course of
his life. At twenty-nine, having just graduated from Ohio Wesleyan
University, he was now faced with two alternatives. The first was to
continue westward to Baldwin City, Kansas, where the offer of a professorship in mathematics at Baker University awaited him. The second
was to remain in Piper City, where only the day before the superintendent of schools had offered him the position of principal at the
comfortable salary of $70.00 per month. It was Sunday, and he had
just gone to church. There remained twenty-four hours in which to
decide whether he should accept the appointment as principal. His
own description reveals how the decision was made:

The cry of my heart was like that of Paul's on his way to Damascus:
"Lord what wilt thou have me to do?" I had no Ananias to tell me, but
I trusted that the Holy Spirit would speak it to my heart. Not far from
the station I sat down on a railroad tie, and thought and prayed. The
question to be decided then and there was: "Shall I accept this offer or
not?" I had not sat there very long, till there was whispered to my con-

3

sciousness as plainly as if it had been spoken in my ear: "Do not accept it."

My decision was instantaneous to obey the voice. . . . Owing to this experience, I never doubted that I had a work to do at Baker.[1]

Thus, with the piety typical of his Methodist heritage, William H. Sweet embarked on what was to be a long and distinguished career as an educator, administrator, and minister in early Kansas Methodism, inspired by no less a charter than a divine calling.

In moving west William H. Sweet followed the example of his own parents, who had moved from Kentucky into Brown County, Ohio, shortly before he was born.[2] There, in a log cabin near the town of Five Mile, he grew up. The home was probably as religious as it was austere and primitive, for his parents were staunch Methodists, his father being an officer in the local church. The major social activity for the family was apparently frequent attendance at the revivals which were common in their own and neighboring counties.

After brief service in the Union Army during the Civil War, William H. Sweet enrolled in Ohio Wesleyan University at Delaware, Ohio, where he met his future bride, Rose A. Williams, who was attending the women's division of the same college. Miss Williams embraced the ideals and principles of her Methodist heritage with a firmness that rivaled her future husband's. Graduating in 1871 as valedictorian of the Ohio Wesleyan Female College, she immediately accepted a teaching position at subsistence salary at Shaw University in Holly Springs, Mississippi, a school for former slaves supported by the Freedman's Aid Society of the Methodist Episcopal Church. Three years later, in September, 1875, she married William H. Sweet and set out with him for Kansas.

The state to which the young couple traveled was in many respects still primitive and uncivilized. The Union Pacific Railroad had spanned Kansas five years earlier,[3] but many areas of the state contained vast stretches of unsettled prairie. Even in the more populated eastern counties, primitive frontier conditions prevailed. Houses made of sod were common sights. Raids by hostile Indians posed a threat to life and property until 1878, by which time Generals Sheridan and Custer had suppressed them. The raucous cowtowns, rail terminals to which Texas cowboys drove their herds to market, were centers of debauchery and lawlessness which seriously threatened the morals and social stability of portions of the state. The forces of law and order were represented by the now famous lawmen James Butler ("Wild Bill") Hickok of Abilene and William B. ("Bat") Masterson and Wyatt Earp of the notorious Dodge City.

These conditions reflect the fact that Kansas was a part of the nation's last frontier during the post–Civil War generation. The Kansas-Nebraska Act, passed by Congress in 1854, opened Kansas to settlement, and the Homestead Act of 1862 gave 160 acres of free land to each settler who was willing to cultivate it. But only with the coming of the railroads did the real settlement begin, for the railroads vigorously advertised the good qualities of the land, often in grossly exaggerated terms. The availability of free land had its intended effect. As the nation recovered from the depression of 1873, settlers began to flood the area. In 1875, when Rose and William Sweet set up housekeeping in Baldwin City, the state census recorded 528,437 persons. By 1880, the figure had almost doubled to 996,096.[4]

Unprecedented prosperity accelerated the population growth. Above average annual rainfall, coupled with an absence of the grasshopper plagues which had periodically devastated the region's crops, produced record yields of corn and wheat. Railroad land advertisements claimed scientific proof that the cycles of drought which had been common to the area were things of the past. Railroad building continued as small branch lines crisscrossed the prairie, an instant boon to the communities through which they passed and the kiss of death to those which were overlooked. Developers arrived to lay out whole new cities along the railroads. Astute land speculators made fortunes. For a time, it appeared as though Kansas was to be a veritable paradise of agriculture and commerce.

Professor and Mrs. Sweet thus spent their early married years in a region which was both primitive and prosperous. They settled in Baldwin City, a town of some five hundred inhabitants, located about forty miles southwest of Kansas City. Sweet continued teaching at Baker University for two years, when it became apparent that his salary at the small school could not support his growing family. He therefore accepted an appointment as pastor of the Methodist Church in Holton, Kansas, another small town fifty miles to the northwest, where he remained for two years. In 1879 he was recalled to Baker University as its twelfth president.

During the seven years of his administration, William H. Sweet transformed the school from a dying institution to one of the largest educational enterprises in the state. With innovative tuition policies, vigorous fund-raising and recruitment, and considerable donations from Sweet's own income,[5] enrollment almost quadrupled from 136 in 1879 to 475 in 1884, and a magnificent new classroom building was erected.[6] Such successes were due in part to the fact that by the early 1880s the Kansas boom was at its height. Railroad construction assumed gigantic proportions, as over five thousand miles of track were laid during the 1880s,[7] far more than the state could efficiently use. The peak year for the farmers was 1881, when the price of corn and wheat reached its highest point between the Civil War and the twentieth century.[8]

In the winter of that prosperous year, on February 15, Rose Sweet gave birth to the third of her six children, William Warren. Little is known of the exact details of his childhood, for he has left us no recorded memoirs. We do know a great deal, however, about his family, his hometown, his region, and the local Methodist institutions which propagated the ideological basis for social values. It is therefore possible, by studying carefully the world in which Sweet lived, to reconstruct the ideas which would inevitably confront the future American historian.

Young Will Sweet's hometown, Baldwin City, had a pronounced religious character from the beginning. It was incorporated in the late 1850s by several businessmen from Palmyra, a village then contiguous with Baldwin City to the north. The area had grown in population because of its strategic location as a stopping place on the Santa Fe Trail, the nation's major east-to-west artery of transportation. As traffic along the trail increased, the location seemed ideal for a large town which, in the minds of its founders, might even become the great metropolis of the West. The founders purchased the land and donated it to the Kansas-Nebraska Conference of the Methodist Episcopal Church on condition that it would establish a college there. Apparently they believed that the presence of such an institution would insure the stability and permanence of the new town. The

Conference agreed and Baker University, named for a pioneer Methodist bishop, was chartered in 1858 as Kansas's first college,[9] financed by the sale of lots in the new town which grew up around it. Baldwin City was thus dominated by Methodist interests from its inception. The town grew slowly at first, its progress interrupted by the Civil War. But when the Leavenworth, Lawrence, and Galveston Railroad was routed through Baldwin City in 1867,[10] its future was assured.

Baldwin City's promoters were quick to capitalize upon the town's Methodist institutions and values. The background for such actions was the prosperity of the late 1870s and early 1880s, which led to a kind of boom psychology in Kansas. Horace Greeley had toured the area in 1859, and after passing through Baldwin City had written home to his *New York Tribune* readers, "It takes three log houses to make a city in Kansas, but they begin *calling* it a city as soon as they have staked out the lots."[11] This propensity for exaggeration reached its peak in the boom of the early 1880s, when all Kansas towns vigorously advertised themselves as ideal places to live. Baldwin City entered the competition for settlers, revealing in its advertisements many of the dominant values of the town. Baldwin City's promoters clearly regarded Baker University as a prime asset. The *Baldwin Criterion* in 1884 anticipated that "under its present teachers many years will not elapse before Baker will not only be at the head of Kansas institutions but will stand second to none in the United States."[12] In 1885, when Will Sweet was four years old, the weekly newspaper printed this jingle:

No whiskey sold in Baldwin. . . .
If you want to educate your family, come to Baldwin. . . .
If you want to live in a town where men never get drunk and fight, come to Baldwin.
We have no billiard halls in Baldwin, and we wont [*sic*] have them which is still better.[13]

These values—prohibition, education, prosperity, social stability—reflect the social complexion of Baldwin City and of Kansas as a whole. The overwhelming majority of Kansans were native-born American Protestants of Anglo-Saxon lineage who emigrated from the band of states extending from Iowa and Missouri eastward to the

Atlantic.[14] The values embraced by these immigrants were clearly expressed in their religion.

Religion in frontier Kansas was overwhelmingly Protestant, dominated by a relatively harmonious coalition of Methodists, Disciples, Baptists, Presbyterians, and Congregationalists.[15] The Protestant coalition grew by means of cooperative revivals[16] and assumed the guardianship of the communities' moral values. Methodists were by far the largest group and often took the lead in moral crusades. They gave impetus to women's suffrage by favoring the ordination of women as early as 1890.[17] Their uncompromising stand on liquor closed many a "joint," as the following account by a Methodist minister illustrates:

The jointists came into the meeting and declared they had quit business and would not resume it. We have a quiet town now. Every joint is closed. An active temperance league stands ready to prosecute the first violation of the law. Sunday hunting, gambling, playing at cards and all games of chance have been suppressed.[18]

The strength and dominance of such a Protestant establishment is further illustrated by the fact that the same coalition caused cigarettes to be banned statewide from 1917 to 1927. This action was but a continuation of the role which these Kansas churches had historically pursued:

In 1886 the legislature ruled against hunting on Sunday; in 1898 a Methodist Bishop urged a campaign against the gum-chewing habit; for playing cards and checkers on Sunday, five men were arrested in Topeka in 1908; during the Kansas Methodist Conference in Topeka in 1915, Reverend Bernard Kelley advocated a law against riding in automobiles on Sunday.[19]

One of the more tangible effects of Protestant hegemony in frontier Kansas was the founding of dozens of church academies and colleges throughout the state.[20] State supported education had not yet come into vogue, and the vast majority of such schools were church sponsored. These institutions made religion the culture bearer of the frontier and placed the Protestant churches which supported them in the center of the effort to civilize the West. Baker University in

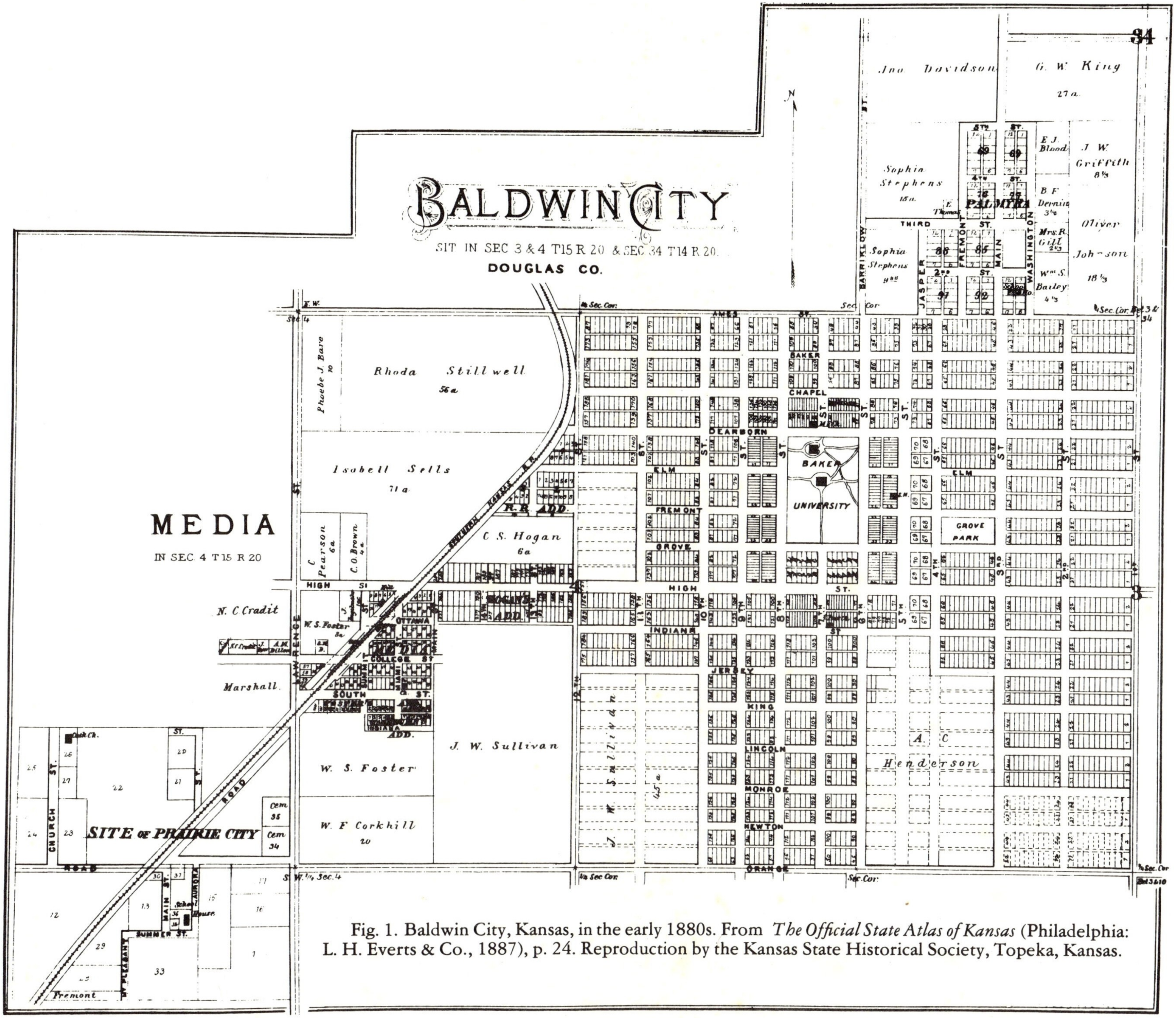

BALDWIN CITY

SIT IN SEC 3 & 4 T15 R 20 & SEC 34 T14 R 20.

DOUGLAS CO.

MEDIA

IN SEC. 4 T 15 R 20

SITE of PRAIRIE CITY

Fig. 1. Baldwin City, Kansas, in the early 1880s. From *The Official State Atlas of Kansas* (Philadelphia: L. H. Everts & Co., 1887), p. 24. Reproduction by the Kansas State Historical Society, Topeka, Kansas.

Baldwin City was the oldest and most prestigious of these institutions. Its presence dominated the town from its inception and played a significant role in making Baldwin City's reputation as the "Kansas Mecca of Methodism."[21]

Baldwin City followed the regional pattern in its ethnic composition. The 933 residents of the town who were counted in the State Census of 1885 included only 40 "colored" and 12 foreign-born individuals.[22] It is likely that the town was over 90 percent Anglo-Saxon, a conclusion which is reinforced by its religious complexion. During Will Sweet's childhood, there were only two churches present. The Methodist Church was the largest, with four hundred members. The Palmyra Presbyterian Church, which later moved into Baldwin City, included only fifteen members.[23] A Roman Catholic Church of some forty members existed in Prairie City, a mile to the west,[24] but it had little to do with the life of Baldwin City. It was never mentioned in the church column of the weekly Baldwin City newspaper. The Methodist Church, by contrast, enjoyed regular weekly attention, and the Presbyterian Church received occasional notice.

The Protestant and Methodist hegemony which provided the ideology of the social structure in Baldwin City was symbolized by the physical layout of the town. In its center stood neither a courthouse nor a business district, but rather Methodist Baker University, the town's social and cultural nexus. The Methodist Church was prominently located on the town square immediately north of the campus. Baldwin City's street were laid out alphabetically and numerically with great care, a model of order and propriety. The regularity and neatness of the town suggests the stability which its founders sought in giving the land to the Methodists. (See map of Baldwin City, Kansas.)

If the weekly newspaper in Baldwin can be taken as representative of the town's values, then it can be said that Protestant religion was viewed as the very foundation of a stable society. When William Warren Sweet was four years old, next to advertisements for corn hullers, steam washing machines, touring phrenologists, and blood purifiers, the newspaper gave its own editorial advertisement of the value of Protestantism in Kansas society:

Our exchanges report revivals of religion in every section of the state.

. . . Whenever the individual is thoroughly reconstructed by the gospel of grace, the spirit of an enlightened Christianity and sound Republicanism, the wheels of material and spiritual industry, prosperity, and power will spin and hum . . . Prohibition and the country are eminently safe under Republican rule . . . On with Prohibition! On with the revivals! Prosperity will follow like magic.[25]

Under the control of the right politics and the right religion, a bright future was envisioned for Kansas. Since Sweet's time, the region's prosperity and politics have undergone considerable flux, but little has changed concerning the dominance of the early Protestant coalition in Kansas, nor has the preeminence of Methodism within that coalition been significantly challenged.

The moral standards which confronted a child growing up in Baldwin City in the home of the president of its leading institution would not be very different from those expected of the students at Baker University. An early college catalog describes the strict requirements:

Punctual and regular attendance at recitation, at public college exercises, at prayer and at church, and observance of study hours are required of every student. Unladylike or ungentlemanly conduct, disrespect toward the faculty, irreverence at church, noise in rooms on the Sabbath, writing upon or otherwise defacing the college building or furniture, using profane language, wearing firearms or other weapons, visiting circuses or theatres, card-playing, keeping intoxicating liquors in the room are strictly forbidden.[26]

It is clear from published records that Sweet's father wholeheartedly embraced the strict Methodist moralism which such rules reflect. A nephew remembered him from his brief stay in Nebraska before he was married, commenting that his

strong Christian character—which he never compromised—was so unusual at that time and place, that it made him prominent, and although I was a small boy then, I can well remember some of the comments about him. Before leaving, he was offered a good position in a bank by the leading banker of Nebraska City.[27]

As might be expected, Sweet's father was a stern disciplinarian, and occasions were not lacking when he boxed young Will's ears.[28]

Such sternness was not obsessive, however, for Sweet's father was also gentle and kind. A Baker student recalled him in a description of the opening chapel exercises of 1880:

. . . the faculty was now filing across the rostrum, the President at the head, and seating themselves with proper form and dignity. Expectant hush in these four walls dedicated to the breadth of ideal Christian education. Then the leading official, Dr. William H. Sweet, stepped to his place to announce the hymns, . . . read the Scripture and offer the eloquent prayer invoking God's special blessing upon this day and all the days to follow, here in his courts.

A man with a bit of gray in his brown hair and full beard, the strong body of medium height carefully dressed in an easy clerical suit, moving deliberately, as became his high calling. Eyes clear and steadfast, probably blue, or maybe gray, that we knew very little later had a glint of humor in them, ready for 'most any turn in his manifold problems. Later on, also, we could depend upon a constant kindliness in keeping with any position. And on occasion a most engaging smile emphasized the strength of mouth and chin through the hirsute barrier of the period. The large nose and shapely ears balanced the broad brow, and it was just good to feel that we had such a well-favored guide and friend.

Naturally as we grew in grace and stature in our general courses, we compared Dr. Sweet with the other members of the Faculty, ten men and two women, through my three years, though there was probably a change or two. And our satisfaction increased in many ways, finding him more and more efficient as our college world broadened into wider possibilities. He was very human. He had some of the faults and failures no man or woman fully overcomes. But he was entirely the gentleman, whatever came, well-balanced, far-sighted, and never too occupied with the big things before him to consider the small things that concerned us. We liked him so much. Preaching the Word in the spirit and understanding. Living the Word at home with his family. And most of all putting each and every student in the way of finding himself, than which no one can do more for another.[29]

If these admiring words are true, the Sweet home must have been a model of frontier Methodism—disciplined but loving, gracious, cultured, and above all, devoutly religious. It must have been a haven for what William Henry Sweet later called "the refining influence of Christianity."[30]

The Sweet family left their Baldwin home in the summer of 1886, when Will was five years old. His father had resigned the presidency of Baker and had accepted a position as professor of psychology and ethics at the newly established Kansas Wesleyan University in Salina, 150 miles to the west. Having built Baker into a successful institution, perhaps he felt there was more need for his efforts in the less settled areas of the region. Although Salina was located in a more sparsely populated area than Baldwin City, the town itself was larger since it was located at the confluence of four railroad lines. By 1886, its population had surpassed 3,000.[31] Professor Sweet remained at Kansas Wesleyan only two years, when economic hardships caused him to abandon his faculty position and accept the pastorate of the local Methodist church. The struggling young college had chosen an inauspicious time to begin its existence, for the Kansas boom had peaked and perilous years lay ahead.[32]

The pastoral assignment lasted two years, after which the Sweet family moved twenty miles north to Minneapolis, a town of seventeen hundred citizens,[33] where father Sweet was again the Methodist minister. The family returned to Salina in 1892 when William H. Sweet was made presiding elder (today called district superintendent) of the Methodist district, a post which he occupied until 1899, the year Will Sweet left home to go to college.

It was during these years that Will began to read. One work which made a particularly strong impression on him was William H. Milburn's *Lance, Cross, and Canoe*,[34] a popular book about the taming of the West. Milburn was himself a circuit-riding Methodist minister in the Mississippi Valley before the Civil War, and his works vividly portrayed the savageness of the untamed frontier and the heroism of frontier ministers, themes which would later appear in Sweet's historical works. Sweet kept a copy of this work throughout his life, cited it and quoted from it in one of his early works,[35] and read it to his children.[36] Another favorite work was Benjamin Franklin's *Autobiography*, which he later gave to his own children.[37] He also enjoyed the Frank Merriwell Series of novels by Burt L. Standish, which complemented Franklin's philosophy by venerating boy-heroes who were models of American virtue and success.

Life in Salina and Minneapolis was in one respect very different from the tranquillity of Baldwin City. The Sweet family still lived

in an orbit that was totally dominated by Methodism, but the prosperity that had characterized the region during the Baldwin City years
vanished in the ten-year drought which began in 1887 and devastated
Kansas's agricultural economy. By 1890, between 75 and 90 percent
of all Kansas farms had become mortgaged; and in the first six
months of that year, ten thousand of those mortgages were fore-
closed.[38] The result of such disasters was widespread social and political
turmoil throughout the Midwest. Angry farmers turned to the Alliance and Populism for a redress of their grievances against a moneyed
eastern establishment which directly or indirectly controlled their
mortgages. Mary Ellen Lease, "the Kansas Pythoness," gave the
agrarian movement its most publicized slogan when she urged the
farmers to "raise less corn and more hell." They evidently followed
her advice and for a few years gained limited control of Kansas
politics..

This agrarian radicalism did not, however, significantly alter the
values of Sweet's social environment. The Alliance and Populist movements were resisted even at their peak by most Republicans and
Methodists,[39] a coalition which probably included Sweet's father.
When Kansas newspaper editor William Allen White printed his
famous anti-Populist essay, "What's the Matter with Kansas,"[40] he
spoke for the broad segment of educated Kansans who were genuinely
frightened at the radical economic proposals of the Populists. The
Salina Daily Republican-Journal echoed White's sentiments in 1899
by calling Populism "the greatest freak of the age." Noting that
"today the Republicans have a majority in the legislature," it proudly
predicted that "the first step to be taken by the Republicans will be
to throw out every law passed by the late Populist legislature. . . ."[41]
The prediction was correct. Populism was short-lived, losing influence in the economic recovery of the turn of the century.

The tragic conditions which led to such political turmoil exposed
Will Sweet to another aspect of frontier Protestantism. During the
prosperous years in Baldwin City, Methodism had been the bearer of
education and morality. During the drought years in Salina and
Minneapolis, the church took on the character of a benevolent institution. Will Sweet's older brother, Paul, described that period as
"among the hardest years Kansas had ever experienced. One of the

recollections of my boyhood was of the barrels and boxes filled with clothing which came to our house, shipped from the East, to be distributed by my father among the needy people of his district."[42]

Sweet's childhood, then, exposed him to prosperity and poverty, social stability and social turmoil; but through all the changes there existed a powerful and constant ideology in the immediate social contexts of family and church. Given the limitations of the available data, the exact significance of a childhood lived under such conditions is difficult if not impossible to assess. It must be remembered that in the most explicit sense we know almost nothing about the early life of William Warren Sweet. However, our knowledge of his parents, principally his father, and of the social contexts in which the Sweet family lived, should enable us to make some generalizations concerning how the world probably appeared to the young future historian.

Sociologists of knowledge have emphasized the crucial role played by primary socialization, i.e., a child's first induction into the social order. This process of initiation necessarily imposes on the child a definition of reality which ordinarily will form the basis for all subsequent intellectual activity.[43] Interaction with subsequent social worlds can modify the definitions of reality acquired in childhood, but for most individuals the childhood world remains "the home world, however far one may travel from it in later life. . . ."[44]

It can certainly be said that William Warren Sweet's primary socialization confronted him with a relatively consistent ideological structure. His childhood and early adolescence were spent in young Kansas towns whose social institutions, ethics, and values were shaped by frontier Protestantism. That this world of the small town had a profound influence on the intellectual development of countless numbers of Americans is undebatable. Thorstein Veblen noted that "the country town is one of the great American institutions; perhaps the greatest, in the sense that it has and had and continues to have a greater part than any other in shaping public sentiment and giving character to American culture."[45]

It is also likely that the influence of such towns was essentially conservative. Page Smith, one of the few historians who have investigated the role of the town in American life, has emphasized this conservatizing trend in the development of American towns. Countering the Turnerian notion that westward migrants were restless liberals dissatisfied with the static conventionalism of the East, Smith shows that many western towns were populated by religious conservatives who could not adapt to the increasing pluralism and secularity of eastern cities:

> The transplanting of Eastern "culture" froze rather than liberated it. The new town "clung to traditional institutional forms and social practices; and it hungered after intellectual and social contact and parity with the East. A large part of western opportunity was the opportunity to imitate an older society." Before the West could claim parity, it had to prove that it could successfully emulate its supercilious parent. The frontier towns were thus an enormously conservative force since they clung tenaciously to "forms" and "practices" that were a generation old by city standards.[46]

The towns with which Smith deals are mostly colonized towns, i.e., towns founded by groups of migrants who, bound together by a common religious faith, left the East to begin life anew together in greener pastures. Although the Kansas towns in which Sweet grew up do not conform in this respect to Smith's colonized model, they exhibit a moral and religious conservatism as strong as any examples which Smith uses. The reason for this similarity is perhaps that Kansas's unusually strong Protestant majority made possible common ideals and values which approximated the religious homogeneity of the colonized towns.

What then was the intellectual heritage which these conservative towns transmitted to William Warren Sweet? The clearest answers to this question lie in Baldwin City, not only because it was Sweet's introduction to the social world, but also because the Methodism of Baldwin City epitomized the Protestant hegemony of frontier Kansas and thus can be used as a key to an understanding of the intellectual structure which dominated Sweet's childhood world. Among the myriad assumptions which social life in Baldwin embraced, several are directly related to Sweet's later career as an American historian. These assumptions are, first, that Methodist and Protestant Christianity was the bearer of the most valid American cultural values; second, that such values separated the civilized and stable communities from the uncivilized and unstable ones; and third, that the goal toward which history progressed was the "civilization" of the frontier through Methodism and its Protestant allies. Sweet's parents held these assumptions and, in fact, organized their entire lives around them. Thus, whether in Baldwin City, Minneapolis, or Salina, the social contexts which most significantly affected the Sweet family remained relatively constant. William Warren Sweet's childhood intellectual world was defined by the fact that he was the son of a Methodist minister and administrator, raised in a home where we may surmise that virtually every guest shared the overriding concern of the family, namely the Methodization of the frontier, or in the words of William H. Sweet's most outstanding Baker student, "the seizing of Kansas for God."[47] Moving to three different but similar Kansas communities during childhood would tend to strengthen the conviction that the world view which they embodied was indeed widely accepted.

As we will later see, William Warren Sweet's rural background was not particularly unusual among his later intellectual contemporaries. What was different with Sweet was that unlike many other academic leaders of his generation,[48] he did little to modify the intellectual heritage of his childhood. In fact, Sweet's later historical theses can be seen as a veneration of the ideology of his early life in Kansas. When he later claimed that American religion was born on the frontier, fed by revivals, and dominated by a grand coalition of Methodists, Baptists, Presbyterians, and Congregationalists, no data could have demonstrated the claim more clearly than the history of the frontier Kansas of Sweet's boyhood days. When he asserted that the church colleges rescued the West from barbarism, Baker University could have been his prime example. When he eulogized the sacrificial devotion of frontier ministers, no more appropriate instance could have been described than the career of his own father. And when he wrote one of his finest monographs, "The Churches as Moral Courts of the Frontier,"[49] no more persuasive evidence could have been marshaled than the brief advertisement in Sweet's hometown newspaper, "If you want to live in a town where men never get drunk and fight, come to Baldwin." Sweet's historical portrait of American religion was a historical reification of his childhood world, almost Baldwin City writ large. Both its strengths and its weaknesses, its genius and its limitations, ultimately derive from this fact.

2

Getting an Education
1895-1911

BECAUSE BOTH OF SWEET'S PARENTS were college educated, it was assumed in the Sweet family that all the children would receive some college training. Thus, after his elementary education in the public schools of Salina and Minneapolis, fourteen-year-old Will Sweet entered the Preparatory Division of Kansas Wesleyan University at Salina in 1895. Here, accompanied by his older brother Paul, Will prepared himself for undergraduate work, helping to pay his tuition with part-time and summer jobs. The Sweet brothers mowed the grounds of Kansas Wesleyan and worked in the hay fields together in the summer.[1] Their close association was to continue until the close of their undergraduate years.

During these years, the Prep School was the most successful of the college's divisions, accounting for half of the total enrollment.[2] Its curriculum was based on traditional educational standards,[3] emphasizing classics and English.[4] If the monthly student magazine, the *Wesleyan Advance*, accurately represents life at the school, then it seems clear that Will Sweet took a back seat during these years to his brother Paul, who was a year older, setting a pattern which was

17

to continue for some time. Paul's name appeared in the magazine on several occasions, mostly as a speechmaker and participant in oratorical contests, whereas the only mention of his younger brother was the terse note, "Why are Will Sweet and Dunmire such great friends of late? If you had been at the last social you would know."[5]

A triumphant optimism characterized the college. During Sweet's four-year tenure, the *Wesleyan Advance* contained numerous articles chronicling Methodist expansion. One article suggested the reason for such growth in terms that Sweet later adopted as his central historical thesis: "It has ever been the policy of the Church so to adapt itself to surrounding conditions and circumstances as to bring them under tribute for the accomplishment of its high and noble aims."[6] A school song described the students of Kansas Wesleyan University as "the boys and girls of all the West, the brightest truest and the best."[7] The town newspaper recounted a meeting of the Kansiana Club at the Presbyterian Church, at which a quartet introduced a new song, "Kansas Land," set to the tune of the revivalist hymn, "Beulah Land."[8]

The mood was enhanced by other movements both regional and national. The literary independence of the Midwest from the East had been militantly declared by Hamlin Garland in Chicago in 1894.[9] Garland called for a new and truly American literature, free of European influence, realistic rather than romantic, growing vigorously out of the midwestern soil. The *Wesleyan Advance* echoed this plea in 1899 in an article entitled "The Kansan in Literature," which claimed, "The Kansan writes as he does everything else, in his own particular and original manner. His themes are fresh. They do not smell of the mouldy past, nor smack of pedantry. He is a pronounced realist and calls things by their true names."[10] The student magazine also demonstrated the growing national mood favoring American imperialism, including its common assumption of Anglo-Saxon superiority. Calling for a broadening of the "too narrow" Monroe Doctrine because "it is simple obedience to the providence of God to do so," and advocating a closer alliance "with that noble English stock from which we sprang," the magazine heartily recommended "the recent counsels of Mr. Kipling," quoting the lines,

Take up the White Man's burden—

> Ye dare not stoop to less—
> Nor call too loud on Freedom
>   To cloak your weariness.
> By all ye will or whisper,
>   By all ye leave or do,
> The silent sullen peoples
>   Shall weigh your God and you.[11]

Its participation in these regional and national movements demonstrates that Kansas Wesleyan University was not culturally isolated; its representatives perceived themselves as a part of larger social contexts. It is thus probable that Sweet's intellectual world was broadened at Kansas Wesleyan, but improbable that its basic presuppositions were seriously challenged. The Methodist and Protestant values of Sweet's childhood continued to provide the ideological basis for the larger world to which he was exposed.

Sweet's academic record in the Prep School does not survive,[12] but the college catalog indicates what courses he would have taken. He is listed as having enrolled in the classical curriculum,[13] which included mathematics courses in algebra and geometry; science courses in physiology, geography, zoology, and botany; history courses in English, Roman, and Greek history; plus regular and heavy doses of Latin, Greek, and English.[14]

The Sweet brothers graduated from the Prep School in the spring of 1898 and remained at Kansas Wesleyan for their freshman year as undergraduates. A year later their father took a pastorate at Beloit, Kansas, and since they could no longer live at home in Salina, they enrolled as sophomores in the autumn of 1899 at their parents' alma mater, Ohio Wesleyan University in Delaware, Ohio. Will and Paul roomed together as sophomores and juniors.[15] They also raised money to pay tuition by working together in the summers selling a medical encyclopedia. They rode bicycles to small towns throughout Ohio, showing *Dr. Chase's Third, Last and Complete Receipt Book and Household Physician*[16] to all who would look. Years later, William Warren Sweet would entertain friends at parties by reeling off the memorized sales spiel.[17] The boys did well enough at this venture to subsidize their college education, with the help of part-time jobs on campus during the school years. In fact, Paul, who was the leader in the project, was able to buy the franchise for the book throughout Ohio. The commissions from later sales more than paid his way through medical school.[18]

During his sophomore and junior years at Ohio Wesleyan, Will Sweet continued to play second fiddle to an outstanding older brother. Paul's name appeared frequently in both the student newspaper and the biennial *Bijou*. He projected the image of the outgoing entrepreneur and clearly reflected pride in his midwestern roots. He served as business manager of the weekly newspaper, the *College Transcript*. He was associate editor of the *Bijou*, which satirized him in an account of a "Bijou Corps Meeting." He is quoted as suggesting, "Let's make it [the *Bijou*] in the shape of a pennant. Wouldn't that be fine? That's the way they do it in Kansas. . . . I'll tell you. Let's have the advertisements all mixed up with the other matter. They'll pay more for them. Wouldn't that be fine? That's the way they do out west."[19] Will Sweet, in contrast, made almost no appearances in school publications in his sophomore and junior years.

By his senior year, however, things began to change. Will Sweet was elected captain of the football team. In his junior year, the team had a losing record, but under the direction of a new coach, the team in his senior year started to win consistently, and Will became a campus hero overnight. After the first game of the season, the school newspaper reported, "Captain Will Sweet, full back, of last year, has the good will of all the men. His record last year has won him the confidence of every one in his ability to lead the team to victory. He had the men out for spring practice and the result is apparent."[20] As the football fever infected the entire campus, Will was courted by several fraternities. Because of the expense involved, neither he nor Paul had joined a fraternity; but finally Will acceded to the urgings of his younger teammate, Branch Rickey, later of baseball fame, and joined Delta Tau Delta, moving out of the little room at 171 West Winter Street which he had shared with his brother for two years.[21] The season closed with a record of seven wins and two losses, with Will receiving weekly plaudits in the school newspaper. The headline after the final game read, "OMU 16—OWU 18," followed by the subheading, "Best Exhibition of Football Ever Seen on Our Grounds."[22] Reviewing the season's accomplishments, another article noted that

"Captain Sweet has been a diligent, hard-working leader, and in this has been an example to all the men."[23]

William Warren Sweet had finally made an achievement independent of his gifted brother which had established him as outstanding in his own right. The competitiveness, energy, and drive evident in this accomplishment characterized Sweet's later life as well. It was said, for example, that he never walked up a flight of stairs; he ran instead, taking steps two at a time.[24] His later personal and family life continued to demonstrate his interest in outdoor sports and competitive games.

Will Sweet's academic training at Ohio Wesleyan was of exceptionally high quality for a denominational college at the turn of the century. During his undergraduate years, Ohio Wesleyan was undergoing a gradual transformation from an older, classical curriculum to a modern program emphasizing the sciences, electives, and history. Such a transformation was common among colleges and universities at the time.[25] Under the direction of the outstanding president, James W. Bashford, these changes resulted in significant improvements in the academic quality of the school.[26] A faculty roster for 1901 includes an impressive number of earned graduate degrees, including doctorates from Tübingen, Halle, Munich, Johns Hopkins, and Harvard.[27] The historian of Ohio Wesleyan concludes that during this period the university was "in the highest position she has ever held among the colleges of the country."[28]

Sweet's undergraduate transcript reveals an excellent academic record. The courses, with the exception of those entitled "Spelling," "Moral Science," and "Rhetoric," are ones which might well appear on the transcripts of today's liberal arts graduates. Sweet took heavy concentrations of language courses (Greek, Latin, Spanish, German) and majored in history, which included courses in the history of Germany, English history, modern history, and constitutional history. As at Kansas Wesleyan, no American history course was taught, that field being still unknown at most institutions. Will Sweet's grades ranged from the mid-70s in his freshman year to the high 80s and 90s in his junior and senior years. If his improved grades are an indication of his intellectual growth, his athletic successes must have been a constructive influence. Ohio Wesleyan had no Phi Beta Kappa chapter during Sweet's tenure; but later, when a chapter was established, he was elected to honorary membership.[29]

The prosperous Ohio Wesleyan provided a contrast in some respects to the primitive and struggling Kansas Wesleyan of Sweet's Salina days. Its buildings and grounds had just undergone renovations and additions in preparation for the Semi-Centennial of 1894.[30] It was much larger, with an enrollment of over fifteen hundred students in all divisions,[31] and more prestigious, counting among its trustees ex-President Rutherford B. Hayes.[32] Student social life was vigorous and varied. Fraternities, social clubs, and time-honored traditions played important roles, in contrast to the absence of such things at the young Kansas Wesleyan. The "new" theories of evolution and higher criticism of the Bible began to find their way into the classroom without the trauma experienced at some denominational colleges. President Bashford himself propounded the new views and recruited faculty with the training necessary to teach them.[33]

Ohio Wesleyan's openness to Darwin and to the critical biblical scholarship of Wellhausen and others in no way inhibited traditional religious fervor or ethical ideals. The furtherance of institutional Methodism continued to be the primary reason for the college's existence. Daily chapel was required of all students. Campus revivals were commonplace. President Bashford himself, in fact, held some of the most successful revivals.[34] Rules against attending theaters, smoking, drinking, and similar breaches of Methodist moralism were strictly and uniformly enforced,[35] a fact which Paul Sweet noted in his later description of the school as "a college where character building held chief place in its curriculum and where more attention was paid to moralities than formalities."[36] These rules appear little different from those of Baker University or Kansas Wesleyan University which William Warren Sweet had experienced in previous years.

The new theories could be accepted without trauma because they did not fundamentally threaten the intellectual structure of Methodism. The denomination's Wesleyan theology was based not on the biblicism which permeated so much of American Protestantism at the time, but rather on revivalism and its goal, the "warmed heart" of a conversion experience. While the views of Darwin and Wellhausen struck at the very roots of those kinds of Presbyterian and Baptist

theology that lay in the rationalistic biblicism of which today's Funda-
mentalists are heirs, they left the basic theology of many progressive
Methodists relatively untouched.

Ohio Wesleyan University thus provided a smooth intellectual
transition for William Warren Sweet. Here his intellectual world was
broadened without being fundamentally changed. Methodism remained essentially what it had been in frontier Kansas, namely, the
bearer of education, the guardian of moral values and social stability,
the ideological cornerstone of culture.

Will Sweet graduated from Ohio Wesleyan in the spring of 1902
and accepted a position as a high school football coach in Fostoria,
Ohio. He occupied the position during the academic year 1902-3 while
he was also attending Ohio Wesleyan's short-lived law school on a
part-time basis. Neither coaching nor law held his interest very long.
The following year he entered Drew Theological Seminary in Madison, New Jersey, having decided to follow in his father's footsteps and
become a Methodist minister.

Drew was one of Methodism's finest educational institutions. Its
faculty held degrees from impressive schools and offered a broad
seminary curriculum covering the areas of biblical studies, systematic
theology, church history, practical theology, elocution, and hymnol-
ogy.[37] Its mood was open and progressive, offering its students during
Sweet's tenure lectures by such well-known figures as Washington
Gladden, Frank Mason North, and Richard T. Ely.[38] Sweet's undergraduate training had prepared him well for seminary studies. At
Drew he compiled an excellent record. His transcript shows not a
single grade below 94.[39]

The years in Madison were important for more than their academic training. During this period, William Warren Sweet met his
future bride, Louise M. Neill. Miss Neill was by all accounts a woman
of striking beauty, varied talents, and great charm. Her parents were
Scotch-Irish immigrants who met and married in New York City.
Her father had died when she was a child, and her mother supported
the family by operating a boardinghouse in Madison. Miss Neill's
major interest was music. When she met Will Sweet, she was attending the American Institute of Applied Music in New York.[40] They
were quite obviously well suited to one another. After their marriage

on May 18, 1906, Louise devoted herself to her husband and his career for over fifty years of happy married life. He often sought her advice on matters of academic politics, and read aloud for her criticism all of his important manuscripts.[41]

Perhaps it was Louise Neill's interest in music which influenced Sweet's choice of subjects for his Drew B.D. thesis, which is the earliest specimen of his writing that has been preserved. It was entitled "The Influence of the German Chorale upon Christian Music." The essay began by contrasting pre- and post-Reformation German worship. Before the Reformation, according to Sweet's essay, the people were "prohibited to sing inside the churches," and had no alternative but to sit "dumb and silent, understanding not one word of the service, having no voice in their worship." After the Reformation, however, the people were "emancipated from Catholic restrictions" and the German chorale, "the people's song," became a Protestant heritage. This development continued in the Wesleyan movement, "which came like a sunburst over England." The essay concluded with an admonition which was to become a theme of Sweet's career, urging Methodists to reap the benefits of a broadened historical perspective: "We Methodists of to-day have fallen heir to a rich heritage, a heritage not of pure doctrine only; but the hymns and music of the ages are ours, for we can lay rightful claim to the music of Luther, Bach, and the Wesleys."[42] Sweet's B.D. thesis showed the potential for clear and synthetic historical writing which he later developed. It also demonstrated the militant Protestantism which occasionally took on the character of anti-Catholicism in his later works.

Sweet's guiding light on the faculty at Drew was Robert W. Rogers, the professor of Hebrew and Old Testament, about whom he spoke often and affectionately throughout his life.[43] Rogers's *History of Babylonia and Assyria*[44] was the definitive work in its field for many years. His Leipzig Ph.D. had trained him in the latest methods of historical scholarship, and through his teaching William Warren Sweet was exposed to a new kind of history. Sweet had majored in history as an undergraduate, but this work was not done under a trained, professional historian.[45] Consequently, his early exposure to history was soon outmoded, for by the time he had received his undergraduate degree at the turn of the century, a revolution in the discipline of history had occurred. American universities, led by Johns Hopkins, had begun in the 1870s and 1880s to introduce Rankean, "scientific" methods of writing history, including the research seminar, critical canons of evidence, and specialized, monographic literary styles.[46] History was becoming less and less the province of the literate patricians of the leisure class, and more the province of the highly trained, critical professional.

Rogers must have whetted Sweet's appetite for the newer methods, because in his senior year at Drew he took an opportunity to learn more about them. Seniors of superior standing were allowed to take up to five hours of courses at either Columbia University or New York University.[47] Sweet chose to enroll at Columbia in William A. Dunning's popular course, "The United States from 1850, with special reference to the Civil War and Reconstruction."[48] Dunning was widely respected as a reinterpreter of the Reconstruction era. He too was one of the new breed of professional historians. His overriding goal, according to one distinguished observer, was to write "'scientific history' which eliminated as far as possible moral judgments."[49] This approach separated him from many of his older northern colleagues who took a very critical, moralistic view of the Confederate South. Dunning's emphasis on objectivity, which permeated the entire infant discipline of professional history writing, appealed to Sweet; his later treatment of the same subject, the Civil War and Methodism, was advanced with identical claims of impartiality.[50]

Sweet's rising interest in the professional discipline of history was gradually inclining him toward an academic career. However, his commitment to the ministry remained constant throughout his life. After his graduation from seminary and his marriage in the spring of 1906, he accepted a Methodist pastorate in Willow Grove, Pennsylvania, a suburb of Philadelphia, where he remained for two years. Here Sweet's first son was born, named after his older brother, Paul. In 1908, Sweet became the Methodist minister in another Philadelphia suburb, Langhorne, where he remained until 1911.[51] After he became a professor, he retained his clerical status and continued to preach occasionally.

Sweet was never the sort of person who could be content with a simple, leisurely life. He was happiest when he had multiple projects on which he could work simultaneously. Hardly had his first pastorate begun when he enrolled in a graduate program at Crozer Theological Seminary. The seminary has since moved to Rochester, New York, and Sweet's academic record there has not been preserved.[52] All that is known is the title of his thesis, "Theories of the Atonement."[53] He received the Th.M. degree after only a year of work at Crozer, in the spring of 1907.

While at Crozer, Sweet also took a course at the nearby University of Pennsylvania under Herman V. Ames, a noted American constitutional historian. He must have found this work appealing, because following his Crozer degree he enrolled as a full-time graduate student at the University of Pennsylvania, while continuing his ministerial work at Willow Grove and later at Langhorne. Much of his early course work was in Semitics, an interest inspired by his former study under Professor Rogers at Drew.[54] But the appeal of modern history was stronger. After two years of full-time work at the university, Sweet received the A.M. degree in the spring of 1909[55] and then decided to focus on American and European history. The major professor in his doctoral studies was Ames,[56] under whom he had taken the first course at the university. He also took one course with the university's most famous historian at the time, John Bach McMaster.

McMaster and Ames were interested in completely different areas of American history (McMaster in social history and Ames in constitutional history), but both men clearly were devotees of the "scientific" history in vogue at the time, which assumed that the duty of the historian was to gather documentary evidence, recite chronologically arranged "facts," and generally avoid interpretive judgments. McMaster's eight-volume *History of the People of the United States*, published between 1883 and 1913, did depart from the normal political and institutional focus of the scientific historians, as Harvey Wish has pointed out.[57] But McMaster's method left him firmly in the camp of the scientific historians, since he believed that "interpretations" inevitably distorted history.[58] Consequently, the chapters of his *magnum opus* were often a patchwork of diverse data and rambling commentary with no unity or coherence. In the apt words of William T. Hutchinson, "McMaster skillfully regiments his facts upon parade, but they do not march."[59] Herman Ames's method was similar.

His major work, *Proposed Amendments to the Constitution of the United States during the First Century of its History*,[60] was literally an elaborate reference work packed full of chronologically arranged facts. It contained very little interpretation and no thesis whatsoever.

William Warren Sweet's doctoral dissertation bore the same stamp. Its stated aim was to describe in a "scientific manner" the role of the Northern branch of Methodism in the Civil War.[61] Its thesis, explicitly mentioned only in the preface, was simply that Northern Methodism aided the Union cause during the war in every region of the country. The early chapters dealt with separate regions, illustrating in each the loyalty and support which the various conferences and other church bodies gave the the federal government. Sweet credited Methodist influence in the border states, for example, with keeping those states in the Union.[62] The later chapters discussed the loyalist activities of Methodist institutions—southern missions, periodicals, the military chaplaincy, and the wartime bishops. The final chapter on Methodist involvement in interdenominational organizations broadened the work beyond Methodism by demonstrating that other Protestant groups had similar concerns and roles during the war. An annotated bibliography revealed the discriminating historical criteria of Sweet's training, criticizing works which were "uncritical" and "highly eulogistic."[63]

The dissertation's method and thesis indicated the direction which Sweet's career as a historian was to follow. Its enumerative method ("the study deals with facts alone")[64] was a legacy of scientific history, each chapter becoming primarily an organized presentation of voluminous historical data, the relevance of which was often left to the reader to determine. We are told, for example, that attending the General Conference of 1864 "were 216 delegates from 49 Conferences, presided over by the six bishops,"[65] yet there is no indication as to why these figures are significant. This veneration of historical data as important for its own sake led Sweet later to edit and publish many volumes of source material in American religious history. The thesis of the dissertation, that Northern Methodism aided the Union cause, may seem all too obvious, but it linked religion with politics in a relationship which Sweet later expanded into an integral partnership between the Protestant churches and American society, the cornerstone of his subsequent synthesis of American religious history.

Sweet had a minor difficulty interesting his fellow Methodists in publishing his dissertation, since it dealt with so controversial a phase of their history. He first sent the manuscript to the Eastern Division of the Methodist Book Concern in New York, which rejected it on the ground that it would open old wounds in the separate branches of the church and become an obstacle to the plan of reunion which was then being considered.[66] After the initial rejection, he sent it to the Western Division of the Book Concern in Cincinnati, where it received a more favorable reading and was published. The incident had a lasting influence on Sweet. For the rest of his life, he was a crusader among Methodists for what he called "historical-mindedness." He asserted that "the only way to deal with the past is neither to attempt to forget it, nor to ignore it, but rather to come to an understanding about it."[67]

Once published, the dissertation received mildly favorable reviews. The best one was contained in the *American Historical Review*. After noting that "the subject is in itself an illustration of the attention which American historians are just beginning to give to the neglected field of church history," the reviewer gave an astute criticism which Sweet would later heed:

> The study is ecclesiastical rather than religious. The author might well have devoted more attention to methods and results of the camp revivals, to an analysis of sermons, and to the reflex effect of the war on church thought. He has, however, refrained from handling questions involving subjective treatment, deterred by a somewhat too narrow interpretation of "scientific" method. He achieves impartiality, but one feels that the cause of historic accuracy would have been even better served if the "mephitic gases" which Professor R. G. Stevenson, who wrote the introduction, refers to as latent in chapter V., had been permitted a few quiet and regulated explosions.[68]

Sweet subsequently devoted considerable attention to these "mephitic gases," especially revivalism, but he never gave up the claim of impartiality and objectivity which was a legacy of his graduate training, even after the concept of "scientific" history had been virtually destroyed in the 1930s and 1940s by the attacks of Becker, Beard, and "Bulletin 54."[69]

Ironically, it was precisely his view of history as objective which kept Sweet from examining critically the assumptions about American history with which he grew up. Because history was conceived as morally and philosophically neutral, a science rather than a creative art, the scientific historians felt no need to scrutinize the presuppositions of their point of view. Some, like John W. Burgess and George B. Adams, went so far as to claim that a historian ought to have no presuppositions and no point of view, but should rather report simply what happened. In such a milieu, Sweet was able to become a highly skilled practitioner of his craft without ever having to recognize and confront, not to mention question, the assumptions of Protestant hegemony which formed the foundation of his construction of historical reality.

The fact that during this period the American academic community in general embraced and embodied similar assumptions concerning Anglo-Saxon and Protestant hegemony surely reinforced Sweet's childhood impressions. Laurence Veysey described the undergraduate population of the time as "remarkably homogeneous: a parade of Anglo-Saxon names and pale, freshly scrubbed faces."[70] Richard Hofstadter noted that "in the Progressive era the primary function of the academic community was still to rationalize, uphold, and conserve the existing order of things."[71] That such an existing order was founded on Protestant ideals and values is beyond dispute.[72] Even the reformers of the day were influenced by Protestantism, for as Hofstadter stated, "The Progressive mind . . . was preeminently a Protestant mind; . . . it inherited the moral traditions of rural evangelical Protestantism."[73]

In other, more specific ways, Sweet's graduate training reinforced the world view of his Methodist youth. McMaster praised the Anglo-Saxons as "the most persevering, the most energetic, the most thrifty of races,"[74] venerated the Methodist circuit rider,[75] and has been called "the first national historian to appreciate the importance of the West."[76] The widespread discussion of Frederick Jackson Turner's frontier thesis during Sweet's graduate years also complemented perfectly the assumptions he brought with him from Kansas and Ohio Wesleyan.[77]

Sweet's higher education thus focused and solidified the intellectual world of his childhood and youth. His years as an undergraduate and a seminarian facilitated personal growth in many ways, but did not bring into question the fundamental values of his earlier home and family life. His training at the University of Pennsylvania, although rigorous by the standards of the time, did little to challenge the world view which he inherited from the small-town Methodism of frontier Kansas. What he did acquire from his education were the intellectual tools with which the unreflective, taken-for-granted world of childhood could be translated into a highly sophisticated construction of American religious history.

3

The Young Professor
1911-1927

AS SWEET MOVED TOWARD THE COMPLETION of his dissertation at the University of Pennsylvania, he was offered a position as an instructor in history at his alma mater, Ohio Wesleyan University. His former history professor there, Richard T. Stevenson, had become vice president of the university, leaving no one to teach the history courses in the curriculum. Sweet accepted the offer and moved his family to Delaware, Ohio, in the summer of 1911, embarking on a new career as school opened for the autumn term.

Sweet was held in high esteem by the administration at Ohio Wesleyan. His suggestions for reorganizing the history courses which he was asked to teach were accepted readily by the president and vice president.[1] When Sweet's dissertation was published, Vice President Stevenson wrote the introduction in which he exhibited great respect for the academic credentials of his former student. He stated,

The spirit and method of proceedure [sic] used by Mr. Sweet are not those of a lauditor, but of the scientific analyst, as becomes the accomplishment of the doctorate of philosophy degree for which he offers this in the University of Pennsylvania. In no sense is he a special pleader. He has

31

not suffered his natural affection for the Church of his fathers to queer his judgment.[2]

Clearly Sweet's "scientific" training as well as his "natural affection" for Methodism made him quite an asset to the Ohio Wesleyan faculty. He was promoted from instructor to assistant professor after his first year of teaching, and then to associate professor after his second year.

Sweet's appearances in student publications at Ohio Wesleyan stressed his involvement in campus athletics. He promoted a student-faculty baseball game in the spring of 1912,[3] and was named graduate manager of athletics beginning in the following autumn.[4] After occupying that position for a year, he was the subject of an article in the college newspaper which revealed something of his personality:

Prof. W. W. Sweet, with his quick snappy stride, has been a prominent figure on Edwards' field all year, and the reason is that his job as graduate manager of athletics requires a close contact with all that is going on or should be going on in the way of football, baseball, tennis, or track.

The visiting teams, it is said, have frequently inquired whether Prof. Sweet was a special officer in citizens' clothes, or the owner of the field and gymnasium, but the professor has always managed to untangle his identity before he has finished his financial dealings with the foreigners.[5]

Sweet's "quick and snappy stride" expressed the authority, confidence, and efficiency with which he took charge of all his tasks. He was the sort of person whose presence typically evoked the question, "Who is that man?"

Sweet's commanding personality and prestigious academic degrees made him attractive to other colleges also. Late in the summer of 1913, officials of a Methodist college in a neighboring state became interested in hiring Sweet for their faculty. DePauw University in Greencastle, Indiana, had a vacancy in its one-member department of history, and sought to fill it with a person possessing the credentials to chair an expanded department in future years. DePauw's president, George R. Grose, dispatched Bishop Edwin H. Hughes to interview Sweet, beginning a chain of events that was to strain the relationship of the two Methodist colleges. The episode reveals details of Sweet's personality and the esteem in which he was held by his colleagues.

Hughes visited the Sweets at their home in Delaware and sent the following telegram to President Grose:

VERY FAVORABLE IMPRESSED REPORTS ABOUT MAN GOOD PERSONALITY FINE MUCH BETTER THAN THAT OF MISSOURI CANDIDATE FEEL CONFIDENT ANY SLIGHT LIMITATION WOULD BE CORRECTED BY CHANGE OF SCENE AND ADDED RESPONSIBILITY . . .[6]

He expanded on his impressions in a letter written the next day: "He has a fine appearance; is interested in athletics; is definitely religious; is said to preach most acceptably at Broad St., Columbus; and is altogether quite beyond the ordinary. I met his wife. She would fit in admirably."[7]

Ohio Wesleyan was predictably reluctant to let Sweet be taken from them. Vice President Stevenson answered an inquiry from President Grose about Sweet with the following remarks:

Sweet is making good—Has fine *health—bearing—character*, and O.W.U. ideals. I think he is approving himself as a teacher, and he is disposed to produce, as you note in the . . . [unintelligible] He is a good preacher—for the present supplying a Presbyterian Ch—near Delaware.

He has been made *Associate* Prof. this year—having been Ass't.

May I suggest that for our sakes as well as yours, you do not disturb him this year—Wait, and if he still grows and deepens, and heightens, then come again.[8]

Grose was not deterred, however. His inquiries continued to elicit glowing reports about Sweet. W. G. Hormell, Dean of Men at Ohio Wesleyan and one of Grose's former professors, wrote Grose a lengthy description of Sweet. In Hormell's eyes, Sweet was a very hard-working teacher, "a judicious grader," and one who "gets good work out of his students." He was "much above the average as a public speaker," and talented in the pulpit, leading chapel exercises "with dignity and always with good effect." Sweet's appearance revealed "a good athletic build and military carriage." Louise Sweet was described as "a charming woman. She has fitted into our faculty circle and we are very much pleased with her." Together, "they are a fine looking couple and are at ease in society."

On the negative side, Hormell noted that Sweet "tells a story well" but "has been criticized for telling one or two stories which some thought were off color." His athletic responsibilities seemed to have brought out some unpopular traits of his dominant personality: "As graduate manager of our athletics he has gotten into trouble with our gymnasium director and also with some of the students. They say he is dictatorial and a little overbearing, and is quick tempered. I suspect these criticisms are just; but the position is a difficult one and he is new at the work." The letter concluded, "There is so much good in him that I confidently expect him to improve in all these lines. I again say that we do not want to give him up."[9]

Other reports quickly confirmed Hormell's remarks. Professor T. G. Duvall of Ohio Wesleyan, formerly of DePauw, described Sweet in a telegram with these words:

SWEET IS GOOD TEACHER, WELL PREPARED IN HIS SUBJECT AND GETS GOOD WORK DONE NEVER HAS OPPORTUNITY TO DEVELOP DEPORTMENT BUT INDUSTRIOUS, AMBITIOUS AND HAS OWN IDEAS, IS RELIGIOUS THEOLOGICALLY CONSERVATIVE AND IN SYMPATHY WITH BEST COLLEGE TRADITIONS STANDS WELL WITH STUDENTS, ACTIVE IN ATHLETICS FINE PRESENCE AND PERSONALITY.[10]

In a subsequent letter, Duvall qualified his one criticism of Sweet by noting that his faults "are such as are generally taken for granted in a young man of energy and ambition."[11] Another faculty member at Ohio Wesleyan and formerly at DePauw was William E. Smyser, who wired President Grose an equally positive recommendation:

FIRST CLASS MAN SCHOLARSHIP TRAINING, TEACHING ABILITY UNUSUAL MENTAL AND PHYSICAL ENERGY KEEPS MANY IRONS IN FIRE PERHAPS TOO MANY UNSETTLED UNTIL RECENTLY BETWEEN PREACHING AND TEACHING SOMEWHAT UNPOPULAR AMONG STUDENTS ACCOUNT BRUSQUENESS SPEECH AND MANNER BUT GENUINELY KIND AND WHOLESOME ACTIVE INTEREST ATHLETICS GRADUATE MANAGER SORRY IF HE LEAVES.[12]

The unanimous recommendations led Grose to invite Sweet to DePauw for an interview, where he was offered a full professorship and the chair of history, at a salary of $1,700 per year, a considerable increase over his salary at Ohio Wesleyan. Sweet wanted to accept, but was concerned about whether he could gracefully leave Ohio Wesleyan so late in the summer and so close to the opening of another term. President Grose therefore took aggressive steps to persuade the administration at Ohio Wesleyan to release him. He wrote Vice President Stevenson,

> I appreciate the embarrassment which we may cause you in disturbing him, especially at this late date. . . . While we regret any inconvenience or embarrassment that you may be caused in the event of his acceptance, of course you will not forget that at the most critical period of DePauw's history in recent years, two of your men, Doctor Duvall and Dr. Smyser were taken from here. Now we only ask that you be neighborly in cheerfully releasing Doctor Sweet.[13]

The remarks failed to secure Sweet's release. Officials of Ohio Wesleyan exerted strong pressure on him to stay. He acceded to their demands and refused the DePauw offer in the following telegram:

> ON CONSULTING AUTHORITIES HERE AND THINKING THE MATTER OVER CAREFULLY I HAVE DECIDED THAT IT IS NOT BEST FOR ME TO CHANGE THIS YEAR IF THE CHAIR OF HISTORY AT DE PAUW WERE OFFERED ME FOR NEXT YEAR I WOULD ACCEPT NOW WILL WRITE PARTICULARS.[14]

Sweet amplified his reasons for declining the offer in the letter which followed. He stated that the administration of Ohio Wesleyan "would have condemned me for leaving at this time," and that they had offered to increase his salary, "very nearly bringing it up to the figure you offered me for the first year." Sweet indicated his willingness to come to DePauw the next year and added, "I feel sure if you knew the feeling here, you would understand my position."[15]

This setback did not daunt the young and ambitious President Grose. He continued to press Stevenson to release Sweet. He secured statements establishing the fact that Ohio Wesleyan had itself made similar offers in previous years to DePauw faculty members Duvall and Smyser, the first in "mid-summer" and the second in September.[16] In each case, DePauw had allowed them to leave. Finally Stevenson relented. In a conference with President Grose in Delaware on August 20, Sweet agreed to come to DePauw immediately, and he began to make plans to move his family there. When the president of Ohio Wesleyan made his annual report to the trustees, the whole incident took on a very amiable tone:

> During the summer Associate Professor W. W. Sweet was asked to become a full Professor of History in DePauw University. From the standpoint of salary, rank, and the particular work to be done, the offer was most inviting, and with the approval of Vice President Stevenson, he accepted.[17]

Sweet could not have asked for a better teaching situation than DePauw offered. Enrollments in history courses had been small under his predecessor, Andrew Stephenson, who, according to the historian of DePauw, "had a reputation which intimidated many of the students."[18] Stephenson had a minimum reading requirement of 2,250 pages per semester for most of his courses, and from their descriptions in the college catalog, some seem almost to have been devised for the express purpose of discouraging enrollment.[19] It is easy to understand why enrollment in history courses increased immediately upon Sweet's arrival and continued to grow throughout his fourteen-year tenure. The historian of DePauw (whom Sweet himself had recruited for the history department) explained that "Sweet's vigorous personality was attractive, and his boundless energy led him into a career of writing, preaching, and lecturing in addition to class work."[20] Within a year he had completely revised the curriculum of the department, expanding the American history offerings from two courses to six.[21] By the time he left DePauw in 1927, the faculty of the department had expanded from one full-time member to five, in addition to two department members who held joint appointments in other departments. Sweet inherited an unpopular, isolationist department which demanded that "the entire work for a major" be done within the confines of its own narrow curriculum.[22] He transformed it into a vigorous and appealing department which encouraged interdisciplinary interests.[23]

Sweet's confidence and energy had their liabilities as well as assets. The annual *Mirage* described him in 1916 with the statement, "Dr. W. W. Sweet is noted as being one of the squarest profs. on the campus and a man who is not afraid to say what he thinks."[24] This outspokenness sometimes got Sweet into trouble. In 1918, for example, Sweet made some critical comments about DePauw in a conversation with several Methodist ministers. Existing records do not reveal exactly what he said, but his remarks were repeated and rumors soon led some to the conclusion that Sweet was disloyal to the university. After a discussion with President Grose, Sweet had to submit the following apology:

DEAR SIR:

Since there has been suspicion aroused among certain members of the North Indiana Conference concerning my attitude toward DePauw University, due to certain conversations which I had with members of the above Conference, I desire to make the following statement:—

Whatever I may have said, or whatever may have been inferred from what I said, I had no thought of disloyalty to DePauw University. If I have been indiscrete [sic] and have thereby done any harm to the institution, with which I am connected as an instructor, I am very sorry.

Very truly yours,
WM W. SWEET[25]

Sweet also offered to resign, but President Grose would not consider it. He wrote Sweet, "We will consider the incident closed. You have had as a teacher and will still have my high appreciation and as an associate and friend my full confidence."[26] The incident apparently was not unique, for Sweet's daughter, Elizabeth, later remembered him as one who always "spoke his mind and was never intimidated by anyone. He confided to me once concerning my mother that she was a wonderful person who put out the fires that he started."[27]

During the DePauw years, the size of the Sweet family was increased with the births of two children. The second child, Elizabeth, had been born during the stay at Ohio Wesleyan. The third, Esther, came in 1915, and the fourth, William Warren, Jr., was born in 1917. Within three years at Greencastle, Sweet's salary had increased to $2,000,[28] and the family was able to afford a spacious house near the college on a large lot of about half an acre. Here Mrs. Sweet, who was especially talented in interior decoration, created a lovely home for her family.

A happy domestic life did not divert Sweet from academic pursuits, for he had a large study at home in which he often worked. The children frequently awoke in the mornings to the sound of his two index fingers pounding rapidly at the typewriter, turning out a speech or article or book. In the late afternoon, he enjoyed cultivating his large vegetable garden. He used gardening and other menial tasks as an opportunity to think about what he was writing. Often he would talk aloud to himself while shaving or gathering vegetables, composing and revising paragraphs of whatever manuscript was on his mind. Then he would come inside, go immediately to his study and close the doors, the signal that he was not to be disturbed, and type what he had just composed. This system worked well except for the time the family cat chose his desk chair in which to have her kittens. His eagerness to compose while doing everyday chores made possible the tremendous volume of books and articles which he eventually produced. One key to his productivity lay in his amazing power of concentration, a measure of his motivation and energy. It was said he could get up from the typewriter in mid-sentence, spank a child, and return to finish the sentence without hesitation.[29]

The fact that he worked constantly, and perhaps compulsively, did not mean that Sweet ignored his family. He spent time each day with his children, putting them to bed for afternoon naps by telling them stories about pioneer children from Milburn's *Lance, Cross, and Canoe*, the same ones that he had read when he was a child.[30] In the evenings, he occasionally gathered the family for prayers, or for the reading of *The Swiss Family Robinson* around the fireplace. Although he could be a harsh disciplinarian, most of the time he was gentle and kind, and he was always devoted to the interests and problems of his family.

A highlight of each year was the summer vacation. Sweet would usually find a teaching position in a summer school for the first half of the summer. The family would accompany him to the new location, spending time touring and exploring new territory while he taught his courses. After Sweet had finished his summer teaching, they would take an automobile trip in their Maxwell until it was time to return to Greencastle to prepare for another term at DePauw. Most of these summer schools were at Methodist institutions, usually headed by a seminary friend of Sweet. The family spent summers in this manner at Cornell College, Mount Vernon, Iowa; Northwestern University, Evanston, Illinois; Syracuse University, Syracuse, New York; and the University of Washington, Seattle. A favorite summer resort was Bay View, Michigan, where the Sweet family often began or ended their vacations.

The DePauw years were busy ones for Sweet. Aside from his full-time teaching load, his increasing duties as a department chairman and a member of the athletic committee, and his growing family obligations, he continued to preach on Sundays for small country churches around Greencastle. During the war years he helped to direct an army cadet training program at DePauw. He seemed to thrive on a busy schedule and a hectic pace. The annual *Mirage* noted in 1917 that "history and Methodism and baby Sweet kept the Doctor hurrying most of the time,"[31] but it did not explain that he probably would have been in a hurry in any case. He found time for leisure too, but he pursued it as he did other activities, with great vigor. He went fishing every week with three other DePauw faculty members, was an avid golfer, and frequently hunted on the farms of his Sunday parishioners.[32]

In spite of all this activity, or perhaps because of it, Sweet published eight books and several articles during his fourteen years at DePauw. In them he began to elaborate the formative concepts in his synthesis of American religious history.

One of Sweet's first important publications after his graduate work was an article which grew out of his dissertation research. It was published in 1915 in the *Mississippi Valley Historical Review*. Whereas the dissertation had dealt primarily with the influence of Methodism in the North before and during the Civil War, this article concentrated on Methodist influence in the South during Reconstruction, focusing on the significant number of Methodist ministers who were elected to political office there. It broadened the seminal ideas of the dissertation in ways that were to become characteristic of Sweet's later writing.

The article began with the central assertion, "The influence exerted by the churches on political conditions was never so potent as during the slavery controversy and the Civil War and reconstruction periods."[33] This insistence on the significance of the churches'

role in American history would be one of the major themes of Sweet's
career. In this article, he confined his claims to the Reconstruction
period only, declaring that "the churches and their activities should
be more thoroughly understood in order to comprehend clearly these
periods."[34]

Sweet's description of the purpose of the article reveals its major
assumptions:

This paper is an attempt to trace the influence of the church, particularly
the Methodist, on the political situation in the South at the close of the
war. The Methodist church has been chosen as the typical example for
the reason that its activities were the most widely distributed and also
because matter relating to that body is more accessible.[35]

Sweet's willingness to speak of "the church" when he meant "the
churches" reveals his assumption that the American churches could
be treated as a monolithic entity. That entity, as will be shown later,[36]
was a highly selective historical construction, excluding as it did such
large religious bodies as the Catholic and Lutheran churches, and it
was unquestionably a Protestant entity. Equally important is the fact
that Sweet regarded the Methodist church as "the typical example" of
his church coalition. He was to place growing emphasis on Methodism's representativeness as he increasingly focused his attention on
the study of Methodist history.

Sweet had not been at DePauw very long when his interest turned
from Civil War Methodism to frontier Methodism. The change occurred somewhat by chance, as a result of his own continued involvement in institutional Methodism. When Sweet had moved to Indiana
in 1913, he had joined the North Indiana Conference, Methodism's
ministerial and administrative body in that region. Through this association he came into possession of the official records of the old
Indiana Conference,[37] which covered the years 1832 to 1844. Sweet
placed these records in the DePauw Library and edited and annotated
them with the help of students in a seminar in early Indiana Methodist
history during the winter quarter of 1915.[38] He persuaded the conference to subsidize the publication costs, wrote an eighty-nine-page introduction, and published the work in 1916 under the title, *Circuit-
Rider Days in Indiana.*

The Conference Journal itself contained minutes of the annual meetings of ministers in the region. At these meetings new preaching assignments were dispensed by the bishop and presiding elders, circuits were revised, ministerial candidates were admitted and ordained, committee reports were heard, financial matters were settled, and disciplinary action was taken. Through these records the administrative policy and growth of the church could be accurately traced. Sweet's introduction to this volume of records was limited to a chronology of local events coupled with occasional descriptions of colorful and dedicated frontier preachers. The descriptions were reminiscent of the accounts which Sweet read as a child in the works of William H. Milburn, although the romantic elements were largely absent. The chronological sections were written in the dull, enumerative style of Sweet's teacher, Herman V. Ames. They were occupied with questions of when the first minister came to a given area, who succeeded him, the size and date of the first church building, how many circuits covered a certain region, and so forth.

Yet there were hints in this work that Sweet would eventually transcend the reluctance to synthesize and interpret which he had imbibed from the archivism of the scientific historians. He noted, for example, that some of the towns which were inhospitable to Methodism had been settled by "criminals from the east and others of criminal tendencies, who found the restraints of the law disagreeable."[39] In other, more fortunate communities, however, "some man of wealth or some family of culture" would "recognize that respect was due to religion, and that its influence on society was decidedly helpful, and they endeavored to promote its advancement."[40] Here we encounter for the first time in Sweet's works an assertion of the fundamental connection between Protestant strength and social stability, prosperity, and cultural advancement, the same connection which the weekly newspaper of Baldwin, Kansas, had eulogized during Sweet's childhood there. As he continued his career, Sweet made this connection more explicit. It was to be the cornerstone of his historical construction of American history.

Another hint at an idea which would later become important was Sweet's statement that "the growth of Methodism had kept pace with the growth of population," and that "the itinerant sysem was pe-

culiarly adapted to the time and country."[41] Subsequently Sweet would
link frontier church growth directly to denominational polity, claiming that Methodists were the most successful of the frontier denominations precisely because of their itinerant system of employing circuit
riders who could serve churches in a number of locations at the same
time.

The publication of these records brought Sweet into contact with
the official historian of the North Indiana Conference, H. N. Herrick,
who was busy preparing a full-length history of the conference. After
Herrick's death in the winter of 1915, the Conference transferred to
Sweet the assignment of finishing the history. He did so during the
following year and the work, *A History of the North Indiana Conference*, was published in 1917. Sweet retained the large section of
conference records, primarily lists of ministers' locations and dates,
largely as Herrick had compiled them, placing them in the second
half of the volume. He wrote the historical narrative portion at the
beginning of the volume himself. Most of it was enumerative and
chronological, but it gave some attention to the social effects of Methodism, particularly its influence on the debates over slavery and
Prohibition.

Sweet's attitude toward Prohibition was exactly what anyone
should expect, given the facts of his Kansas upbringing and continued
Methodist affiliation. He and his closest associates had always been
teetotalers. At DePauw, the university rules against dances, theaters,
and cards were sometimes violated,[42] but faculty and students alike
remained firm in their traditional resistance to liquor in any form.
When a group of Greencastle merchants succeeded in calling a "wet
and dry" election for December 29, 1913, a date when the DePauw
students would be away from the city for Christmas vacation, the
students countered with a campaign of their own. Of the 121 eligible
voters among the students, 113 returned early to Greencastle pledged
to cast "dry" votes, insuring that DePauw's surroundings would remain "dry."[43]

Such an uncompromising attitude had long been characteristic of
Methodism. During Sweet's DePauw years, however, the attitude grew
in popularity outside Methodism as a result of the increasingly powerful Progressive movement. Most modern observers find it difficult to

consider Prohibition as anything but a political or religious anomaly. Actually it was viewed by many at the time as a sound and intelligent social reform measure.[44] The national acceptance of this traditional tenet of Methodist moralism could not but increase Sweet's conviction that Methodism and its Protestant allies had indeed stamped American culture with their impress. It was thus on a note of great optimism that Sweet concluded his *History of the North Indiana Conference*:

> As this book goes to press the news has reached us of the passage of a prohibition bill by the Indiana Legislature, by a substantial majority in both houses. Of the various influences, which have contributed to this happy result, none have been more important than the Methodist Episcopal Church.[45]

The values and attitudes which Prohibition symbolized were basically the values and attitudes of Sweet's Kansas boyhood,[46] values which he continued to embrace long after the decade of national Prohibition. He remained a teetotaler until his death, and as late as 1947 referred to the repeal of Prohibition as "a tragic error."[47]

Sweet's interest in frontier Methodism grew. He published a third and then a fourth volume of frontier church records based on material housed in the library of Ohio Wesleyan University. The records were minutes of annual ministerial conferences, including data very similar to that contained in Sweet's previous works. The third volume contained the Journal of the Western Conference, covering the period from 1800 to 1811 in the area west of the Alleghenies, including portions of what are now Mississippi, Tennessee, Kentucky, Ohio, and Indiana. The period was one of great Methodist growth, due largely to the herculean efforts of such conference ministers as Francis Asbury and Peter Cartwright. The fourth volume contained the Journal of the Ohio Conference, covering the years 1812 to 1826.

Sweet had tremendous difficulty in motivating Methodist publishers to publish this significant historical material. He regarded their reluctance as an ignorant rejection of an important denominational heritage, as well as a tragic failure to utilize history as a means of intellectual growth. In this spirit, he published an article entitled "The Indifference of Methodists to their Past,"[48] continuing the crusade among Methodists for "historical-mindedness" which began with his efforts to have his dissertation published. Finally, as a result of the article's appearance, he found a wealthy patron in Boston, George H. Maxwell, who agreed to subsidize the publication of the material.[49] The two volumes were published with similar historical introductions in 1920 and 1923, entitled respectively *The Rise of Methodism in the West* and *Circuit-Rider Days along the Ohio*.

The introductory chapters of both of these works testify to the further development of Sweet's historical method. There were still the lengthy sections of factual data whose only interpretive framework was its chronological organization. But each also contained synthetic sections of increasing length which broadened the significance of the work beyond the narrow bounds of its institutional data.

The synthetic sections show for the first time in Sweet's works the influence of Frederick Jackson Turner's frontier thesis, which was being widely discussed among historians at the time. In formulating his thesis, Turner had reacted against the view of American history represented by his own teacher at Johns Hopkins, Herbert Baxter Adams, a view which held that American political and social customs were chiefly of German origin, imported through British institutions. Proponents of this view characteristically focused on the Atlantic seaboard and especially on New England as the cradle of American democracy and egalitarianism. Turner, however, claimed that "the true point of view in the history of this nation is not the Atlantic coast, it is the Great West."[50] He held that "American democracy is fundamentally the outcome of the experiences of the American people in dealing with the West,"[51] and, attacking the Teutonists, claimed that American democracy "was not carried in the *Sarah Constant* to Virginia, nor in the *Mayflower* to Plymouth. It came out of the American forest, and it gained new strength each time it touched a new frontier."[52] According to Turner, the effect on the pioneer of free land in a wilderness environment promoted "individualism, economic equality, freedom to rise," and a host of other typically American traits, thus in the process producing American democracy.[53] In essence, Turner's frontier worked through what Richard Hofstadter has called "a form of geographic determinism."[54] The frontier was the primary actor, molding the people and institutions which invaded it.

Sweet was never, in the strictest sense, a Turnerian; but he did wholeheartedly support one aspect of Turner's approach, namely, the shift of attention away from New England and the Atlantic seaboard toward the West. In fact, he used the popularity of Turner to enhance the significance of his own works on frontier Methodism. He began the first chapter of *Circuit-Rider Days along the Ohio* by quoting both Lord Bryce and Turner on the importance of the trans-Allegheny frontier. He then made the important connection which was to guide the major works of his career: "To what Mr. Bryce and Mr. Turner have said about the West being the most characteristically American part of America, may be added the statement equally true, that the most Methodist part of America is the region west of the Alleghenies . . ."[55] Based on the propositions that the Mississippi Valley was both typically Methodist and typically American, Sweet took the further step of asserting that Methodism and its Protestant allies played a dominant role in *making* the region typically American. Here, of course, he departed radically from Turner, for he ascribed to Methodist influence virtually everything that Turner ascribed to frontier influence.

In *The Rise of Methodism in the West*, for example, Sweet compared the influence of the circuit rider in the West to the influence of the Jesuit missionaries in the early history of Canada.[56] He pointed out that the circuit rider often "reached the emigrant before the roof was on his cabin or the clay in the stick chimney dry."[57] He noted that these pioneer Methodist ministers stood for law and order, temperance, egalitarianism, education, and genteel manners, and claimed that they successfully transmitted all these traits to western society.[58] Here we find made explicit for the first time in Sweet's works the central idea which was so clearly expressed in the newspaper of his hometown, the idea that Protestant Christianity, typified in Methodism, was the defender of democracy, the guarantor of social stability, the foundation of morality, the provider of education and manners—in short, the bearer of American culture.

Thus, while Turner's main concern was the influence of the frontier on American institutions and culture, Sweet's interest was in the influence of a particular set of institutions, the Protestant churches, on the frontier. Turner saw the frontier as a source of optimism, strength,

and vitality to the American character. Sweet tended to see it as a
dark, moral wilderness which desperately needed to be tamed and
civilized through the institutions of Protestant Christianity. In a paper
read before the American Historical Association in 1922, Sweet concluded, "Whatever may be said in criticism of the frontier Churches
—and there is much that may be said—this much can be said in their
favor: but for them and their work the early American frontier would
have undoubtedly sunk into barbarism."[59] Sweet saw this potential for
barbarism most clearly expressed in the moral standards of some
frontier communities. In *The Rise of Methodism in the West*, he
pointed out that "western morality was extremely loose," but noted
that "in the face of this looseness the Methodist Church maintained
and proclaimed an unbending morality."[60]

If Sweet had been a strict advocate of the Turner thesis, he would
have discussed primarily how the frontier changed existing religious
institutions. Instead he was concerned, perhaps in part unconsciously,
to show just the reverse, namely, how religious institutions changed
the frontier. To be sure, Sweet never ruled out the influence of the
frontier upon religion, and sometimes he spoke of frontier influences
as though he were a disciple of Turner.[61] But he fundamentally dis-
agreed with Turner's economic determinism[62] and, therefore, could
never fully accept the frontier thesis. He did agree with Turner's
focus on the frontier as the stage upon which the drama of American
history occurred. He used Turner's conclusions about the importance
of the frontier to enlarge the significance of his own work. He also
adopted Turner's vocabulary, inheriting in the process some of
Turner's weaknesses, notably the lack of a single, clear definition of
the term "frontier." But the basic argument of the Turner thesis, that
"the existence of an area of free land, its continuous recession, and the
advance of American settlement westward, explain American development,"[63] was only incidental to Sweet's view of history because it left
out Sweet's fundamental causal reality, the structures and religious
dynamic of Protestant Christianity. Sweet did not divorce that reality
from its frontier environment, but neither did he claim that the
environment alone was determinative.

What Turner's concept of the frontier did for Sweet was to provide him with a setting which perfectly explained the institutional

success of American Methodism and its Protestant allies. In *The Rise of Methodism in the West*, Sweet noted that "the other sects moved westward toward the Mississippi as fast as any number of their adherents formed part of the emigration thither, but Methodism alone exercised a weighty influence upon . . . the great unchurched crowd."[64] The effects of this early growth continued to be felt in Sweet's own time, for Methodism was still the largest Protestant body. Thus, in an effort to explain the contemporary dominance of Methodism, Sweet pointed to the earliest setting in which that dominance appeared, the frontier. He stated,

The Methodist plan of organization was exactly suited to a new country and a scattered population. Frontier society was in a state of flux, but the ministers of the Methodist Church were equally mobile and were just as much at home whether society were on the move or stationary. It seems probable that no other system could have met the conditions; at least no other did.[65]

In addition to its polity, the theology of the Methodist church was also remarkably compatible with the frontier, for the circuit rider

preached a gospel of free grace, free will, and individual responsibility. He brought home to the pioneers that they were the masters of their own destiny, as opposed to the Presbyterian and Baptist doctrine of predestination and foreordination. Methodist theology thus fitted in exactly with the new democracy rising in the West, for both emphasized actual equality among all men.[66]

Here Sweet characteristically adopted Turner's concept of the nature of frontier society, while remaining silent on Turner's concept of the primal role of the frontier environment in producing that society.

Actually Sweet could have used his data to contradict the argument of the Turner thesis at one of its weakest points, namely, its failure to recognize the significant continuity between the institutions of frontier and nonfrontier society. Sweet could have argued that both the polity and the theology of Methodism were born in England, not on the American frontier. Even the vaunted idea of the circuit rider, as Sweet later admitted,[67] was adopted from Wesley. Thus, the frontier success of Methodism could be seen as an indication that the insti-

tutions of frontier society did not take on their characteristic traits
from a frontier environment, but instead brought those traits to the
frontier from a nonfrontier setting. Sweet moved in this direction
when he noted that "the natural tendencies and hardships of frontier
life were insurmountable handicaps to organized religion."[68] Turner
himself recognized that the aims of frontier religious institutions were
not entirely in harmony with the emancipating effect of the frontier;
on the contrary, the churches represented efforts to repress or "regu-
late" this effect.[69] Nevertheless, Sweet never directly confronted the
Turner thesis as an adversary. He did later criticize its determinism,
while continuing to venerate the frontier as influential in the development of revivalism and the camp meeting. Sweet thus used Turner's
concepts entirely to his own advantage without committing himself
to the arguments that supported them. He remained free to speak
both of the influence of the frontier on the churches and of the influence of the churches on the frontier.

The publication of the four early volumes dealing with frontier
Methodism, particularly *The Rise of Methodism in the West*, therefore
delineated both Sweet's similarity to and his difference from the dominant American historical model of the time, the Turner thesis. In
the context of reacting to that model, Sweet broadened his historical
method to include more synthesis and interpretation than his graduate
training had allowed. In the process, he arrived at the formative idea
which was the basis for his later historical synthesis of American
religion. That idea assumed Turner's concept of the nature of frontier society, using it as a kind of Darwinian "testing ground"[70] on
which the fittest churches, those best able to meet the needs of frontier society, survived and prospered, while those less fit became weaker
or died. Focusing on the role of the churches in this frontier environment led Sweet to the fundamental and today obvious thesis on which
his later construction of history was based: American religion and
culture influenced each other and, indeed, were interdependent.

In order to support such a thesis, Sweet had to broaden his scope
to include historical materials from more than a single denomination.
Two works which he published during the latter DePauw years began
to expand his focus beyond Methodism. The first was a paper which
he read at the annual meeting of the American Historical Association

in 1922 under the title of "Some Salient Characteristics of Frontier Religion," and later published in the *Methodist Quarterly Review*. Here he first noted that "the three Churches which, more than any others, attempted to meet the peculiar needs of the frontier were the Baptist, the Methodist, and the Presbyterian."[71] Taken together, these three denominations represented for Sweet frontier religion. In his later works, Congregationalism was added as a fourth denomination within the Protestant coalition, the growth of which was the focus for his synthesis of American religious history. In this article, Sweet discussed the similarities and differences in the denominations' roles on the frontier.

The major similarity was the widespread use of revivalism as the primary technique for church growth on the frontier, a similarity made possible by the fact that all three groups held a conversionist theology. Other elements common to Sweet's coalition derived from adjustments to frontier conditions—the use of the camp meeting, extemporaneous preaching, and as an antidote to the loose morality of the frontier, the advocacy of "an unbending morality."[72]

The dissimilarities among the denominations involve their polity and the finer points of their theology. The Baptists and Presbyterians, as Sweet had pointed out in *The Rise of Methodism in the West*, held Calvinistic views of the utter sovereignty of God, predestination, and a limited atonement. The Methodists, on the other hand,

were Arminian in their theology, proclaiming free grace and free will. They taught that man was the author of his own destiny and that his salvation depended largely upon his own will and intention. Such doctrine was seemingly much more acceptable to the frontier, where life was on an equality, where there were no elect in everyday life, and where each individual was largely dependent upon his own efforts.[73]

Presbyterian and Baptist polity was as ill-suited to the frontier as their theology tended to be, for "their ministers were generally settled in one community, serving never more than two or three congregations at most."[74] Methodist polity, however, included the brilliantly devised circuit system, by which a single preacher could serve the needs of numerous communities. Thus, while all three denominations outstripped their competitors as a result of the use of revivalism, the ecclesiastical machinery of Methodism enabled it to grow fastest of all.

This early paper reveals the maturing of Sweet's synthetic ideas. Having decided that the frontier was the proper focus for the development of American religion, having immersed himself for almost a decade in the denominational source materials, and having arrived at a few key theses that plausibly explained the eventual shape of the coalition which occupied his attention, he was ready to construct a general historical account of American religion. His first opportunity to do so came when the Board of Sunday Schools of the Methodist Episcopal Church asked him to write a brief book which could be used to introduce young people to the major American religious bodies. The 135-page book appeared in 1924 as *Our American Churches*.

The first four chapters of the book traced the early history of American religion, beginning with the colonial period and ending with the great frontier revivals of the early nineteenth century. A fifth chapter, outlining the basic types of church government, was followed by seven individual chapters on the major American religious groups. A final chapter discussed the history of church union movements in the United States.

Although Sweet included a chapter on Roman Catholicism, he continued to focus his attention on the growth of the Protestant churches. He began by noting that "the discovery of America and the beginning of Protestantism are contemporary events. As time passed, these two great historic events came to be more and more closely connected in their historical significance."[75] According to Sweet, the formative event in this process occurred in the national period. He described it in a brief section entitled "American Christianity following independence":

One of the outstanding characteristics of American Christianity following the gaining of independence was the rapid growth and extension of what might be termed the popular and democratic churches. The churches that more than any others attempted to meet the peculiar needs of the new communities in America were the Baptist, the Methodist, and the Presbyterian. Perhaps the reason for the more rapid extension of these three churches was the fact that they were considered more democratic

than the older churches of the seaboard; therefore, they made a larger
appeal, especially to the American frontiersman.[76]

Sweet's Protestant coalition thus came to be termed "the popular
and democratic churches." He explained their common strength by
their common adoption of revivalism, and their relative numerical
strength by the degree to which their polity and theology conformed
to the needs of frontier society, using the same ideas which he had
elaborated in "Some Salient Characteristics of Frontier Religion" two
years earlier.

In the separate chapters on specific denominations, Sweet revealed his opinions concerning their role in American history. Of
the three great "democratic churches," Methodism was most successful on the frontier and therefore "the largest factor in shaping the
ideals of the great Middle West."[77] The Presbyterians had the best-
educated ministry,[78] while the Baptists "led the way in the battles for
religious and civil liberty."[79] Congregationalists fared well in Sweet's
eyes because they "introduced pure democracy in America."[80] The
Episcopal church had an influence "much greater than its numbers
would indicate." In the midst of the great variety of new and old
American churches, it "kept a vital connection with all that is good,
inspiring, and beautiful in the past."[81]

It is significant that the Episcopal church is perceived as the
American link with traditional Christianity rather than the far larger
and older Roman Catholic church. Sweet in fact had great difficulty
composing something positive to say about the Catholic church. His
attitude was expressed in the barbed statement, "Lord Baltimore was
undoubtedly a true Catholic, but he was likewise a tolerant and public-
spirited man."[82] Here Sweet merely manifested a prejudice which was
common to individuals of his background. Although he deplored
nativist and other anti-Catholic organizations, he stated that Protestant
suspicion of Catholic parochial schools was "not altogether unde-
served."[83] Unlike the growth of frontier Protestantism, the rapid
Catholic growth in this country was "due almost entirely to immigration," and it is in the area of controlling its immigrants that Sweet
saw a significant contribution to American life. He wrote, for example,
this left-handed compliment:

The Catholic Church represents authority, and its people have the habit
of obedience. . . . we can be grateful for the great moral influence exercised by the Catholic Church over millions of people. The great immigrant hordes that have been pouring into the United States for more than
a hundred years would have been a much more serious menace but for
the control exercised over the majority of them by the Catholic Church.[84]

Sweet did not think highly of the Lutheran denominational family,
either. It suffered because of "its large membership of foreign-speaking
people."[85] Consequently, it "has yet to make its greatest contribution
to the religious life of America."[86] Of the smaller denominations,
Sweet venerated the Disciples for their democratic organization and
for showing that a church could succeed on the frontier without a
credal statement. He commended the United Brethren and the
Quakers for their leadership in social reform movements.

With the publication of *Our American Churches*, the outline of
Sweet's construction of American religious history was firmly established. As we shall later see, he never significantly altered that outline.
His later works, though more sophisticated and more numerous, were
simply elaborations of the same scheme, tracing the rise to dominance
of the three "democratic churches" through their early success on the
frontier. The churches of which Sweet is most critical in *Our American Churches* are the same ones which he criticizes or ignores in his
later works; likewise, those which he most lavishly praises are those
which occupy his primary attention in his later works.

In addition to the five major works dealing with American religious history, Sweet published three other books during his fourteen-year tenure at DePauw. One was a centennial history of Greencastle,[87] largely enumerative and chronological, and of little significance other than as a local history. Another was a very brief
survey of all of Western civilization, also enumerative and chronological, written jointly with his colleague, George B. Manhart.[88] The
third was *A History of Latin America*, written in 1919 as a text for
his course on the same subject at DePauw.

Sweet had taken graduate work in Latin American history at the
University of Pennsylvania, so he was at least familiar with the major
secondary literature in the field. He wrote his Latin American history
simply because there was not an already existing text suitable for

undergraduates. It was a 283-page synthesis tracing the political history of each of the Latin American republics from colonial days to the twentieth century. It was severely criticized by specialists, one of whom referred to Sweet's "evident lack of familiarity with the real literature of the subject."[89] Yet as the same scholar admitted, the work was "the first of its kind to be published in the English language,"[90] and because it filled a need as a textbook, it sold well and was again published, in a revised edition, ten years later.

The work showed the influence of racial concepts common to the period, the same concepts which shaped the immigration restriction laws of the 1920s. The basic assumption underlying such concepts was a theory of inherited racial differences which divided mankind into different groups of subspecies. As Oscar Handlin and others have shown, this kind of thinking was by no means unusual at the time.[91] It was commonly used to advocate the position that "peoples of southern and eastern Europe were inferior to those of northern and western Europe."[92]

A central thesis of Sweet's work was that "at the beginning of Latin colonization in the New World certain characteristics had become definitely fixed in the Spanish and Portuguese character, and the marks of these peculiarities may be clearly traced in the Latin American of to-day."[93] The explanation for these traits lay in the fact that the people of the Spanish peninsula were

the most Oriental of all the European peoples, made so by the free mixing of the blood of the Jews and the Moors with that of the Spanish race, especially during the early medieval period. Thus we must not think of the Spaniard and the Portuguese as we would think of the Frenchman or the Englishman, as being pure Europeans, with purely European traits, but we must think of them as at least partly Oriental.[94]

Oriental traits were seen most clearly in Latin America in "the small white population which rules."

They are full of imagination, far more so than the North American. They are likewise much more sentimental and impulsive. They have high ideals, which they seldom succeed in putting into practice. They are an exceedingly polite race, . . . and their family life is most affectionate. . . . Human life is held cheap among them.[95]

The common people, however, were different from the ruling class. They were dominated by "a very large half-breed, or mestizo class," the product of "the mixing of the Spaniards and Portuguese with the native Indian population."[96] Sweet describes this group as though they had inherited the worst traits of both of their racial ancestors:

> The weak points in the character of the South American may be summed up in these words—mutual distrust, excessive pride, self-indulgence, indolence, and want of persistence. . . . They seem almost incapable of working together in a common work for the common cause. . . . The South American seems to have no shame about giving up. They are good beginners but poor finishers, and the sneer of "quitter" is never heard. A recent traveler in South America has noted the great number of unfinished monuments in Bolivia, an indication of this characteristic, or rather failing, of the Latin American.[97]

Sweet acknowledged that these traits were not the exclusive result of heredity, however, by ascribing their perpetuation partly to an environmental influence. This influence was the Catholic church, which he described as a "chief enemy of education" and a consistent opponent of religious liberty. He claimed, "The Church wants the peon to remain in ignorance so that the priest may continue to exploit him."[98]

Sweet's views on Latin American races and religion are significantly related to his views about the United States. It is difficult to assess precisely the function of his racial thinking in his works on American history because he seldom explicitly used racial categories in them at all. Certainly he never spoke the racist language of the most extreme Nordic supremacist, Madison Grant, or even of the more moderate Henry Pratt Fairchild.[99] The fact that religious categories were the prime evaluative factors in most of his works makes it even more difficult to discover the exact function of the racial categories which he clearly used in *A History of Latin America*. Perhaps his negative evaluations stemmed more from his consistent prejudice against Catholicism than from an assumption of Anglo-Saxon superiority. Certainly he never explicitly claimed that Anglo-Saxons possessed an inherited superiority to other races, and he was a definite opponent of blatantly racist ideologies.[100] Yet the fact that he used the racial categories of the Nordic supremacists in *A History of Latin America* cannot simply be ignored, especially since the Protestant coalition which Sweet characterized as "typically American" was also exclusively composed of predominantly Anglo-Saxon, British-derived denominations. There is in addition the evidence of his occasional use in other works of categories which could have racial as well as religious implications. For example, he once ascribed to immigrants from eastern and southern Europe a corrupt materialism. He claimed, "Those regions in the United States where materialism is most in evidence are those regions dominated by people recently from Europe; and in those regions where there has been the least contact with Europe, there you will find preserved the largest emphasis on the life of the spirit."[101] Whether such a statement is a judgment based on racial or religious criteria may be ultimately impossible to determine. At least it can be said that *A History of Latin America* illustrates Sweet's use of racial categories which are perfectly consistent with his veneration of three Anglo-Saxon denominations as "typically American."

Another significant statement from Sweet's work on Latin America dealt with the conditions necessary to bring about national unity. Having already criticized the social divisions in the Latin American nations, Sweet pointed toward a solution. "Latin America as a whole has many races and many castes," he noted, "and to procure the best results in a republic, unity of race, language, and ideals must somehow be achieved."[102] This kind of unity is precisely what Sweet later claimed as the legacy of his Protestant coalition in the United States.

As with most of Sweet's publications, the book on Latin American history led him to even greater involvement in the affairs of Methodism. His reputation as a Latin American historian resulted in his appointment as a member of the Methodist delegation to an interdenominational missions conference in Montevideo, Uruguay, held in the summer of 1925. He took the opportunity to tour the continent, traveling to Methodist mission points through Brazil and Argentina, then across the Andes Mountains to Chile and up the West Coast. While in Peru, he contracted pneumonia and was critically ill for several days. After he recovered, he returned to the United States and lectured widely about his travels.

Sweet's rising prestige during the DePauw years brought repeated inquiries concerning positions at other institutions. In 1919, a representative of Kansas Wesleyan University wrote President Grose to ask about Sweet, "What kind of college president would he make?"[103] A spokesman for Baker University asked the same question in 1922.[104] Syracuse University offered Sweet a professorship in history in 1923. He described its attractions in a letter to one of DePauw's benefactors, Roy O. West:

One of the most attractive things about the Syracuse position was the larger library and the chance to do work with more advanced students. DePauw, I realize, will always be a college, with few graduate students, but I do feel that our library might be made much more adequate than it is at present. I am not complaining of the present library situation, but only stating that a larger library is attractive to me, for it means the opportunity of doing more effective research work.[105]

Sweet eventually turned down the Syracuse offer, but the fact that he almost accepted it illustrates the kind of position that would most tempt him to move. The next offer was the presidency of West Virginia Wesleyan University, which came in December, 1925. After pondering the offer for over a month, he finally declined, preferring to remain in teaching and research rather than to go into administration. His preference was not honored, however, because the following spring he was made dean of the College of Liberal Arts at DePauw. It was during this period, with the prospect of increased administrative duties taking him away from his primary interests, that an offer of another position came which he could not refuse. It was exactly what he wanted.

The offer came in the spring of 1926. Sweet has left us with a vivid description of the incident:

In the late afternoon of a beautiful Indiana spring day a Cadillac drew up before our house and a tall gentleman alighted. I mentioned the Cadillac because none of my friends were driving cars of that make at that time. At once I surmised that something unusual was in the wind. And there was. This tall, lithe gentleman proved to be Shirley Jackson Case, and within fifteen minutes he had offered me a professorship in American church history at the University of Chicago. There had been no correspondence about the matter, and I was not aware that the University of Chicago had ever heard of me. When I suggested that it seemed rather sudden and that he probably did not know much about me, Dr. Case remarked, "We know all there is to know about you."[106]

Case stressed that Sweet's task at Chicago would be to guide the development of an entirely new professional discipline, the historical study of American Christianity. He would be expected to build up the library in American church history, and was challenged to make it the best in the country. Case promised research assistants and secretarial help so that he could collect and publish source materials in the field.[107] Sweet did not accept the offer immediately because the decision to leave Greencastle, where his career was secure and his family happy, was not an easy one. After he had been dean for several months, however, the Chicago offer looked more and more attractive, and he well knew that such an opportunity would not come to him again. Thus, in the autumn of 1926, at the age of forty-five, Sweet agreed to go to Chicago the following year.

When Sweet left DePauw, the formative years of his thinking were behind him. He never significantly altered the basic outline of American religious history which evolved in the publications of the DePauw years. All he lacked in order to develop this outline into a more sophisticated and integrated historical synthesis was the intellectual stimulation of a highly competitive, graduate level, academic community. Such stimulation is exactly what the new position provided. The Divinity School of the University of Chicago would encourage Sweet to develop and popularize the insights produced by his frontier background, native talent, first-rate historical training, and early research efforts.

4

The Chicago Years
1927-1946

THE SWEET FAMILY spent the summer of 1927 in Seattle, Washington, where there were relatives and a summer school assignment. They returned to Greencastle to pack their possessions, and then set off for Chicago. Sweet's son, William, later described the painful departure:

> I can remember distinctly the occasion of our getting into the car to drive to Chicago. It was in September and extremely hot, and we left Greencastle with heavy hearts and much crying. I think that at that point my father and mother felt that they had made a bad mistake in accepting the appointment; but my father was not one to change his mind, so he offered what encouragement he could and off we went.[1]

The inducements to leave Greencastle were powerful indeed. First, there was the opportunity to join the faculty of a university whose prestige unquestionably ranked it among the very best in the country. Second, there was the appeal of holding the first professorship in the history of American Christianity ever inaugurated, of gathering the formative source materials, and of training the first group of graduate students in the field—in short, the appeal of developing a professional discipline.[2] Finally, there was the prospect of an income increased by more than 80 percent to $6,500 per year.[3]

In spite of these attractions, the first year in Chicago proved difficult for Sweet because of the traumas involved in uprooting his family from the security and happiness of their small-town life. Chicago provided the Sweets with startling contrasts to Greencastle. Son William, who was ten at the time, recalled, "We knew nothing about big city life and had no desire to live in one."[4] The major crisis of the first year in Chicago was obtaining a place to live. Housing was hard to find and very expensive by Greencastle standards. Complicating the problem was the fact that Sweet was very conservative with his money. He had always paid cash for everything, for example.[5] Even though his salary at Chicago was much larger than at Greencastle, it was far from easy to adjust to a considerably higher cost of living.

It took several weeks to find an adequate apartment in Hyde Park, the community surrounding the university. Upon coming to Chicago, Sweet rented two tiny apartments in an apartment hotel for his family, which by this time included three children—Elizabeth, fifteen; Esther, twelve; and William, ten. Paul, who was twenty, stayed behind in Greencastle where he was a student at DePauw. A heat wave kept temperatures during their first week in Chicago over 100 degrees each day, and the small apartments were most unpleasant. The nights were so uncomfortable that Sweet and the children slept on the beach of Lake Michigan. Finally, after several weeks of searching, he decided to rent a three bedroom apartment at 57th Street and Kimbark, a short distance from the campus and directly across the street from an elementary school which Esther and William attended. Compared to their spacious and relatively inexpensive home in Greencastle, it was indeed, in William's words, "cramped and inadequate."[6]

As Sweet became more secure in his new position at the university, he gradually adjusted to his larger income and was less reluctant to spend money. After his youngest child, Richard, was born in the winter of 1928, he decided to buy an apartment in the Cloisters, a luxury apartment building at 58th and Dorchester. Dean and Mrs. Shirley Jackson Case also took an apartment there. The family of

another of Sweet's associates, the Wilhelm Paucks, lived across the
hall from the Sweets. In the Cloisters, the Sweets entertained faculty,
friends, and students with a hospitality and graciousness that characterized all their subsequent years in Chicago.

Shortly after moving to their new apartment, Sweet made another
investment which was to enrich his family life. Through Case
he learned about an old New Hampshire farm which was for sale.
Sweet bought the property as a summer home for his family and
friends and spent every summer there for over twenty-five years.
"Woodlawn," as the farm was called by the Sweets, became for Professor Sweet what his garden had been in Greencastle, a place to relax
and mull over ideas while engaged in menial tasks. There he culti-
vated a gigantic vegetable garden and fruits and berries of many
kinds. Guests were always greeted with a bounteous table crowded
with a great variety of the foods grown on the premises. Summers at
Woodlawn were family affairs, and often all the Sweets adopted a
joint project which required cooperative effort, such as roofing their
100-foot barn, repairing fences, or cultivating up to ten acres of produce for market. Almost everyone who knew the Sweets well—
students, colleagues, relatives, or friends—enjoyed the hospitality of
the farm at one time or another. The Sweet children still speak of
Woodlawn with warm memories, for it was for all of them a haven
from the tensions and limitations of a big city.

Sweet's leisure time in Chicago was spent primarily with faculty
members. He played billards regularly at the Quadrangle Club and
golfed often with his friends Wilhelm Pauck and Fred Eastman of
Chicago Theological Seminary, a Congregational school located on
the campus of the university. On the evenings when Sweet was not
working, he and Mrs. Sweet often socialized with their neighbors the
Paucks, playing their favorite parlor game, Parcheesi.

Sweet's involvement in the affairs of institutional Methodism took
less demanding forms than at Greencastle. The supply preaching
which he had done since graduate school ceased as he spent more and
more time on academic projects. He remained active in a local con-
gregation, St. James Methodist Church, and tried unsuccessfully to
make it more a part of the university community.[7] He occasionally
accepted one-week appointments at Methodist pastoral training insti-

tutes during the summers,[8] and was the faculty advisor to the Methodist study group at the university.

Family life in the Sweet home was little affected by the move to Chicago. The faculty at the University of Chicago may have been more sophisticated than that at DePauw, the Cloisters more comfortable than the Greencastle house, and the neighborhood more opulent, but the Methodist ideals around which the Sweets organized their lives remained constant. While there was little explicitly religious training given the Sweet children at home, Sunday churchgoing was an accepted routine. Prayer and the reading of the Bible were encouraged, but not forced. Perhaps the clearest indication of the continued presence of Methodist values was in the enforcement of a strict sabbatarian ethic upon the children. William Jr. described the home environment of the Chicago years:

We received religious training as children, although it was not to the extent that you might expect. We had family prayers and were made very conscious of the role of religion in our lives, and the discipline was still Puritanical and reflected itself in such things as rules which prevented us from engaging in any athletic or other idle pursuits on Sunday. The most strenuous thing we were permitted to do on Sunday was to take a walk, which we usually did. We were not permitted to play cards, listen to the radio, or even play the piano unless it was a hymn or some classical work. We went to church each Sunday, and each of us was expected to go to Sunday School and then attend church as a family group. At that time we were members of St. James Methodist Church. We had only one automobile, and since our schedules were different the children usually went to Sunday School on the street car and then rode home in the automobile after church. We had a Sunday dinner each week which was always a festive occasion, and we always had something special and more bountiful than on most occasions. As for my mother, she was a religious person but by nature and not by training. Surprisingly enough, none of the children took to formalized religion with any great enthusiasm. This may have been because of our strict Puritanical upbringing, which made us think of Church as a difficult taskmaster. We were not required to read the Bible or to study it, although we were encouraged to do so; and I remember reading it regularly and understanding little.[9]

Thus Sweet's children came to have a very different relation to organized religion than had their father or grandfather.

THE DIVINITY SCHOOL AND ITS RESEARCH PROJECT

Sweet's academic work at Chicago was dominated by the vast project which he was recruited to supervise, namely, the gathering and publication of source documents relative to American church history. The project had had a long history which revealed much about the ethos of the Divinity School and about the state of the historical profession at the time.

The sources project evolved in the context of a general awakening within the historical profession to the importance of the role of religion in American history. The records of the American Historical Association show that the awakening began around the turn of the century. One of the first indications of the change was a paper given by the distinguished historian James H. Robinson in 1899. Robinson criticized the reluctance of American historians to include religious elements in their general American histories. He claimed that such an omission was "the most conspicuous defect in our instruction in general history."[10] In 1900 George J. Bayles echoed Robinson's conerns by calling on historians to write about American religion in a way that did not make history subservient to denominational interests.[11] In 1906, the American Society of Church History was revived as an organization separate from the American Historical Association and free from prejudice against the value of religious history.[12] One year later, Simeon Baldwin gave his presidential address to the American Historical Association, entitled "Religion Still the Key to History," emphasizing religion as one of the major motivating forces in history.[13] In the following year, 1908, J. Franklin Jameson's presidential address before the same body marked the climax of the awakening. He emphasized the wealth of unused social and cultural data to which the historian of American religion had access, stating, "He who would understand the American of past and present times, and to that end would provide himself with data representing all classes, all periods, and all regions, may find in the history of American religion the closest approach to the continuous record he desires."[14] Jameson closed his remarks with a vigorous appeal for historians to look more closely at religion as a key to the development of American culture:

In every other period of recorded time, we know that the study of re-

ligion casts valuable light on many other aspects of history. Why should
it be otherwise with the religious history of America? Unless we are
content to confine ourselves to the well-worn grooves of constitutional
and political history, and to resign to sciences less cautious than history the broad story of American culture, why should we not seek light
from every quarter? Most of all let us seek it from the history of American religion, in the sum total an ample record, even though in parts we
have to compose it like a mosaic from fragments of unpromising material.[15]

During the decade in which Robinson, Bayles, Baldwin, and
Jameson were encouraging colleagues to consider more seriously the
role of religion in American history, a young professor of New
Testament history spoke to the American Historical Association's Conference on the Teaching of Church History on the topic, "The Stimulation of Research." The professor was Shailer Mathews, later to
become dean of the young Divinity School of the University of
Chicago. The Conference Report noted in an obscure sentence one
of Mathews's suggestions which was later accomplished at Chicago
under his leadership: "For the advancement of learning in this field
Professor Matthews [sic] advocated a systematic undertaking to edit
and publish documents of American church history, the work to be
done by instructors and advanced students in collaboration."[16] When
Mathews became dean of the Divinity School in 1907, he had an
opportunity to implement this proposal.

Mathews's tenure as dean extended from 1907 to 1933. During
this period, both the Divinity School and the university of which it
was a part grew enormously in prestige until both were widely recognized as graduate institutions of the highest rank.[17] It is impossible
to understand the spirit which Mathews gave to the Divinity School
throughout his tenure without some reference to the indomitable
optimism which he shared with almost all other religious liberals
during the Progressive era. This mood was captured in the evolution-
ary and progressive thesis of Mathews's *Spiritual Interpretation of
History*, which claimed that

there is discernible in history a basis for interpreting social development
as a passage not only from the simpler to the more complex form of
social organization, but also from occasion and control by impersonal

forces and economic wants to the spiritual freedom which lies in inner self-direction toward spiritual ends.[18]

He epitomized the attitude of many Wilsonians when he asserted during World War I that out of that conflict there would emerge "a nobler social order and a more complete embodiment of the Christian religion."[19] Even war itself was "a survival [of earlier times which] we shall yet outgrow."[20]

Inspired by such buoyant ideas, Mathews succeeded in attracting to Chicago a brilliant faculty which reflected his own view that religion was an integral part of society and therefore ought to be studied in the context of its social environment. He also believed that the empirical and inductive methods of scientific history, when properly pursued, would separate the essential elements of the Christian faith from their particular manifestations in individual societies and would enable modern man to use them most fruitfully.[21] Mathews's "sociohistorical method" became the hallmark of what is now known as "the Chicago school" of historians and theologians, a remarkably prolific and gifted group of scholars.[22]

One of Dean Mathews's first official acts was to appoint Andrew C. McLaughlin, chairman of the history department in the university, to serve concurrently as chairman of the department of church history. McLaughlin was a distinguished American constitutional historian and later president of the American Historical Association who believed strongly in the importance of church history as a specialized branch of scientific historical studies. Under his leadership, the Divinity School's department of church history became more integrated with the university history department. Within a few years, McLaughlin had such well-known historians as Conyers Read, William E. Dodd, and James W. Thompson teaching courses in the Divinity School, even though their primary appointments were in the history department.[23] The annual *Announcements* of the university gave further evidence of McLaughlin's changes.

Soon after taking over McLaughlin dropped the old introductory statement which was concerned solely with church history *per se* and replaced it with a paragraph which stated that since church history was only a "special field" of history it would be wise for students to take some courses in the general History Department. By 1918, seven courses from that department were listed in the Department of Church History.[24]

Thus under the direction of this "secular" historian, the department of church history at Chicago exhibited the dissolution of an older view of church history. In the nineteenth century, as Henry W. Bowden has shown,[25] church history generally had been the province of the seminary professor who conceived of his subject as the manifestation of the providential activity of supernatural forces. Hence church history had to be separated from other kinds of history which dealt with only natural phenomena and ordinary human institutions. McLaughlin, however, brought church history out of its academic isolation and insisted that church historians were distinguishable from other historians only in the particular human institutions which they had chosen to study. They were to use the same tools and methods as other historians, and their conclusions would be judged by the same criteria to which all historians were subject. This thrust followed the guiding philosophy of the first president of the university, William R. Harper, and that of Dean Mathews as well. These men believed that although the Divinity School should function as a seminary, training ministers for the parish, it should exist as an integral part of the university and should—especially in its doctoral programs—maintain academic standards no different from any other graduate branch of the university. Thus the church historians trained under McLaughlin's leadership at the University of Chicago came to be recognized as possessing the same skills and standards as historians trained in any first-rate graduate institution.

Like Mathews, McLaughlin was a thoroughgoing Progressive, with Progressivism's characteristic optimism about the continuing moral, social, and spiritual evolution of mankind.[26] Intimately bound up with this optimism was a view of American history which placed the United States and its democratic ideals in the forefront of human progress, assuming that the rest of the world would eventually follow the American pattern.[27] This outlook encouraged McLaughlin and Mathews to follow the advice of J. Franklin Jameson and others to develop the neglected discipline of American religious history. After all, if the United States was the vanguard of spiritual progress, its religious history deserved careful study. Hoping to develop this field, they acquired one of their own students, Peter Mode, as an instructor in church history in 1916. Mode had written a dissertation in medieval English history,[28] but was interested in modern and American topics as well. In addition to teaching courses in medieval, Reformation, and modern European religious history, he shared the American church history assignments with various professors from the history department.[29]

Mode's interest in American studies grew, and with Mathews's and McLaughlin's encouragement he published in 1921 the first comprehensive sourcebook in American religious history.[30] The work consisted largely of already available denominational records, organized for the colonial period along geographical lines and for later periods along denominational lines. It was an excellent selection of source materials, the only one of its kind for forty years.

Two years later Mode published *The Frontier Spirit in American Christianity*,[31] a brief book of tightly knit essays developed in the course of a series of seminars on frontier religion which he had given at the Divinity School since 1917.[32] These essays marked him as a definite Turnerian. Claiming that "at important stages in the career of our nation, frontier reactions and influences supply the only true understanding to the course of events,"[33] Mode asserted the thesis "that the Americanizing of Christianity has been the process by which it has been *frontierized*."[34] He attributed to frontier influences the following characteristics of American Christianity: missionary involvement, revivalism, founding of denominational colleges, multiplication of small sects, church cooperation and rivalry, centralized church government, and a lack of sacerdotalism.

Mode's essays on the frontier were the charter of an academic career which seemed indeed promising. He had been greatly influenced by Mathews's and McLaughlin's Rankean desire to collect all extant historical source materials on American religion. His sourcebook was a step in this direction, but since it presented no truly new material, it hardly scratched the surface of what needed to be done if a complete record were to be assembled. Mode himself recognized this fact, noting,

Much of the literature that needs to be studied before our frontier religious history is thoroughly understood, lies obscured and unknown in
the attics of the homes of church pioneers who are rapidly passing away.
Much, unfortunately, has been destroyed. Too great haste cannot be made
to accumulate surviving records in convenient centres in order that the
work of investigation may be carried forward.[35]

Mode stood ready and eager to undertake this project if the financial
resources to accomplish it could be found. For a number of years, the
Divinity School simply lacked the funds to fulfill this vision of
Mathews.

In 1923, a noted professor of early church history at the Divinity
School, Shirley Jackson Case, began taking over McLaughlin's duties
as chairman of the church history department. Case's view of history
was in many respects identical to Mathews's and McLaughlin's.
He too was an advocate of scientific history, emphasizing inductive
reasoning based on empirical data.[36] By this time, the term "scientific
history" no longer implied a reluctance to generalize and interpret,
as it had in the late nineteenth century. Neither Mathews, McLaughlin, nor Case subscribed to what Higham has termed the "rigid fac-
tualism"[37] of the earlier American advocates of scientific history, such
as those under whom William Warren Sweet was trained at the University of Pennsylvania. Instead, they followed James Harvey Robinson and other Progressive era advocates of "the New History" in
calling for broader generalizations about the past which were more
relevant to the present and more understandable to the common man,
for closer cooperation with the emerging social sciences, and for a
scope widened beyond institutions to include their social contexts.[38]

Thus Case was free, like Mathews, McLaughlin, and almost all
proponents of the New History, to discern a general pattern in the
entire sweep of human history, namely, "the stately progress of
society's evolution."[39] Even the later ravages of a worldwide depression
and a second world war could not shake Case's pervasive optimism.
He wrote in *The Christian Philosophy of History* (1943): "It is the
duty of modern man to add to the achievements of the ancients, to
make themselves not only the equals but the superiors of their ancestors. . . . Thus history, which is in constant motion, may be marked
by progressive development."[40]

Case administered the department of church history in perfect congruence with such an attitude. The guiding vision behind his administrative genius was his goal to make the University of Chicago the leading American center for research and graduate study in church history. He believed that the time was ripe for Chicago to seize the leadership in the field. He described his ideas in a letter to President Burton shortly after his appointment as chairman in 1923, requesting that his department be enlarged with the addition of a medievalist:

MY DEAR PRESIDENT BURTON:—

May I present to you somewhat informally my most recent meditations regarding the Department of Church History, of which you appointed me chairman not long ago? . . .

The status of Church History research in the world of scholarship today seems to me to be in a very unsatisfactory condition. Apparently the leadership furnished in this field by the German universities in prewar days has passed away for the present, and perhaps for several generations if not forever. French scholarship is so dominantly Roman Catholic that not much help can be hoped for from that quarter. The English and Scottish universities will undoubtedly remain conspicuous for scholarship of a particular type, but probably their work will continue to be limited by a strong emphasis upon tradition. Aggressive leadership in this field of investigation would now seem to be the peculiar duty of the graduate theological schools of America.

It is, however, an unfortunate circumstance that the schools in America have as yet gathered so relatively little momentum to carry them forward to a position of leadership at this time. The scarcity of teachers of Church History in America has been strikingly emphasized by the way in which successors to lately retired or deceased teachers have been chosen. The position left vacant at Yale by the death of Professor Walker has been filled by the appointment of a young man who took his Ph.D. degree at Yale not long ago in the New Testament field. The Church History chair of Professor Emerton at Harvard has passed to another New Testament man, Professor Lake. Similarly, at Rochester Moehlmann, a New Testament man, succeeds Rauschenbusch. My own semi-transition, which antedates each of the above instances, was evidently an early sign of the times. While we may feel like congratulating ourselves on the success of New Testament study in producing this overflow, nevertheless I think we must recognize that from the standpoint of economy in time and efficiency in equipment it would have been more desirable to have had men who had from the first been trained in the field of their later work. It would seem very clear that graduate theological study in America during the last generation had been giving altogether too little attention to the subject of Church History.

In thinking of Chicago as the place where such study may be pursued most effectively in the future I have in mind the following considerations:—

(1) The close affiliation between the work of the Department of Church History in the Divinity School and the graduate work in History in the University. This state of affairs already established with us more adequately, I believe, than at any other institution offers great privileges to the student of Church History.

(2) The prestige already enjoyed by our school in consequence of the position held by students who have specialized with us in Church History. I have in mind, for example, Holtom of the Baptist Theological Seminary in Tokyo, McNeill of Knox College, Toronto, Dadson of Brandon, New of McMaster, Allison of Colgate. These teachers direct students toward Chicago rather than to any other school.

(3) The general policy of the University in providing not simply a staff sufficient for teaching the classes but also a sufficient number of teachers for carrying on adequate research work in the principal divisions of a department. No other theological school in America is, I think, so fortunately situated as ours in participating in this ideal of the University.

If our Department of Church History is to function as it should during the next generation in training leaders in this field it seems to me that there is one missing link in our equipment that needs to be supplied at an early date [namely, a medievalist]. . . .

In a word, do we not need a third man on the faculty . . . who will be responsible for this at present neglected section of the field? . . . In view of the large opportunity which seems open for the development of Church History study in America during the next decade or two, and believing that our own school should take a leading part in this development, I am naturally very anxious that our department should be strengthened in the direction above indicated.

Yours very sincerely,
S. J. CASE[41]

When John D. Rockefeller, Jr., gave one million dollars to the endowment fund of the Divinity School in 1925,[42] Case was given the resources to begin implementing his plans.

One of Case's major research interests was the gathering of source materials on American religion which Shailer Mathews had called for in 1904. Professor Peter Mode had already begun work on the project[43] when he hastily resigned in the winter of 1926 in the wake of a divorce scandal. This tragedy was the occasion for Case's recruitment of Sweet.

When Sweet came to the Divinity School in the autumn of 1927, he joined a group of young but established historians who had been brought together by Mathews and Case and who were united in their concentration on the social contexts in which religious institutions arose. This emphasis was of course Case's *forte*.[44] Besides Case, who taught the period to A.D. 800, the church history department included, after 1928, Professor John T. McNeill, who specialized in medieval and European topics; Winfred E. Garrison, who concentrated on the Renaissance and Reformation periods; and Sweet, who taught the American courses. Associated with them were Matthew Spinka and Wilhelm Pauck of Chicago Theological Seminary, who covered the Eastern Church and the Reformation, respectively; and Charles H. Lyttle of Meadville Theological School, who dealt with topics in modern church history. By the time Sweet and McNeill joined the department it constituted "the largest group of church historians working together in a single department to be found anywhere in the United States, if not in the world."[45] This group gradually became known as the "Chicago school" of environmentalist historians, a phrase which accurately describes their common interest.[46]

In keeping with their characteristic insistence that religious movements be studied not only as discrete institutions but also in the broader context of their social and cultural milieu, the tenured members of the department changed their titles. They no longer wished to be designated as professors of church history, since that term implied a focus on a particular institution. In 1925 Case requested that his title be changed from professor of early church history to professor of the history of early Christianity. Similarly, Sweet arrived in 1927 with the title of professor of the history of American Christianity, and McNeill came in 1928 as professor of the history of European Christianity.[47]

The presence of so distinguished a group of scholars motivated by the high goals, superlative standards, and confident leadership of Professor Case gave the department of church history an aura of excitement and adventure. Case and his department led a kind of reformation within the American Society of Church History, of which Case had become president in 1924. Case's biographer described the sad state of the organization when Case was elected:

At that time, this group was moribund, as near dead as an organization could be and still live. It had less than a hundred members; its publications had lapsed or appeared only on rare occasions; it was limited by charter to the state of New York, met yearly in the metropolis of that state, and was controlled by the professors of church history of the theological seminaries in that immediate area.[48]

When Sweet arrived at Chicago, he joined Case in vigorous efforts to resuscitate the organization. In 1932, Sweet too served as the organization's president. Case and Sweet led membership drives which successfully broadened the constituency of the society and gradually made it into a truly national organization with especially strong support in the Midwest. A research committee was formed, and Sweet served as its first chairman. In 1931, the society's journal, *Church History*, was founded. Case, Spinka, and Sweet petitioned the American Council of Learned Societies to grant membership to the American Society of Church History.[49] Annual meetings of the society began to be held for the first time regularly in the Midwest. These efforts to seize the reins of the society were often opposed by society leaders in the East, and sometimes the efforts of the Chicago historians took on the character of a direct challenge to eastern leadership. In a letter to Sweet, Case criticized the program for the annual meeting of 1932 as "of the same character as usual. Apparently Loetscher picks up what he can in the vicinity of New York and ignores the rest of the members when it comes to making up the program for the annual meeting."[50] In another letter to Sweet from the same period, Case referred to the present as "a time when we are trying to break loose from the New York fetters."[51]

The church history department at the university also became active in an organization known as the Church History Club, a group of church historians from the several seminaries and theological schools in the Chicago area. With Case's encouragement, the University of Chicago professors began attending the regular monthly meetings. Later they encouraged their advanced students to attend. Meetings were held at a downtown club, and it became quite an honor to be asked to present a paper to the group.

The intellectual stimulation which this kind of academic setting produced in the department of church history at the university could be seen in the increasing number of graduate students which it attracted, as well as in the sheer volume of publications which it produced. Case's department was responsible for publishing over twenty books during his tenures as chairman and later as dean, which together spanned fifteen years.[52] The most prolific member of the department was without question Professor Sweet, who wrote seven volumes in his eleven years under Case's administrative supervision.

When Sweet came to Chicago, he immediately plunged into the research project for which he was recruited. The first phase was to locate the source materials. He contacted librarians and denominational leaders soliciting their help. He wrote, for example, to the editor of a Disciples of Christ journal: "We are making an attempt to gather materials at the University of Chicago bearing on the history of all the churches of America. We are searching for manuscripts, rare books, letters, and diaries. The University plans to publish some of the manuscripts which seem of the most value."[53] During Sweet's first academic year at Chicago, he made numerous journeys to colleges, denominational archives, historical societies, and seminary libraries to locate and catalog material.[54] The kind of painstaking work which this initial phase of the project entailed can be seen in Sweet's own description of one of his research trips:

I have just returned from an extended trip to New York, Washington, and Philadelphia, where I looked over much manuscript material. I went over the duplicate pamphlets at Union Theological Seminary and selected about five hundred or more for our library. In my opinion it is a "gold mine." I spent two days at the Congressional Library and we are sending our secretary within a few days to make photostat copies of materials there. I also spent a day in the Pennsylvania Historical Society at Philadelphia and made a list of all manuscripts relating to the history of American churches there.[55]

Later Sweet employed dozens of alumni of the Divinity School to search for and copy unpublished manuscripts.

As the materials began to be located, they were carefully cataloged on large file cards which eventually numbered several thousand. Dean Mathews encouraged Sweet to devote his full energies to the project. He wrote, "I beg of you, do not overload with teaching. We have got too many big projects on hand for you to get tired out."[56] Within three years, initial decisions had been made about the organization of the published documents, editorial work had begun in seminars directed by Sweet, and Case began to solicit a publisher for the first volume.[57] Henry Holt and Company agreed to publish it, and in 1931 *Religion on the American Frontier*, Volume I: *The Baptists 1783-1830* appeared.

Case wrote the general introduction to the series, explaining its purpose and significance:

> Convinced that important documents might soon be lost beyond recovery, the Department of Church History in the Divinity School of the University of Chicago has undertaken systematically to locate and collect these original sources for the history of Christianity in America. One can easily imagine how much more complete and valuable the so-called *Ante-Nicene Fathers* and the earlier parts of Migne's *Patrologia* would have been if the materials had been comprehensively assembled a few decades after the events instead of centuries later. An enterprise of this sort cannot be too early undertaken or too comprehensively conceived. Even when it is possible to print only a selection of documents, the effort may stimulate wider interests in the discovery and preservation of such historical records. With these ends in view a series of volumes containing original sources for the history of Christianity on the American frontiers has been projected.[58]

The original publication plans called for division of the published volumes into two groups, the first including materials gathered east of the Mississippi and the second including materials from the region west of the Mississippi.[59] As the project grew, it became apparent that neither the time nor the resources would be available to complete both groups, and the plans for the western volumes were eventually dropped. A few western documents were included in the final volume of Methodist sources.

The volume of Baptist sources was well received, but it did not sell as well as Holt had hoped. An official of the company wrote Sweet five years later wanting to dispose of the five hundred remaining copies.[60] Holt refused to publish the second volume without a subsidy,[61] but Harper and Brothers was willing. Thus Volume 2 of *Religion on the American Frontier* appeared in 1936, subtitled *The Presbyterians 1783-1840*. It too failed to be a money-maker, and the remaining two volumes in the series, *The Congregationalists* (1939) and *The Methodists* (1946), were published by the University of Chicago Press with subsidies provided by the Divinity School.

Each of the volumes in the series consisted of an introduction of approximately one hundred pages, followed by several hundred pages of documents organized both topically and chronologically. The introductions contained several chapters outlining the institutional history of the denomination during the early national period, stressing the themes of geographical expansion and numerical growth. The general thesis which united all of this interpretive material was of course that those churches which were institutionally most successful on the frontier became and remained the biggest and best in later historical periods. This thesis formed a basis for all of Sweet's synthetic works about American religion.

The documents which occupy the bulk of the volumes in the series were indeed a major contribution to historical scholarship. They included congregational records, missionary diaries, autobiographies, testimonies, and letters, virtually all of which were previously unpublished. They remain without question the single most important group of sources relative to the history of Protestantism on the American frontier. As one reviewer correctly noted, "Professor Sweet is opening a gate through which many succeeding scholars will gratefully pass."[62]

Yet the series had serious weaknesses, flaws which were characteristic of most of Sweet's works. In the first place, the series ignored two major religious bodies, Catholicism and Lutheranism, not to mention the scores of smaller groups which had a role in frontier society. Secondly, by focusing on the frontier, the volumes left the impression that what was occurring in the cities or in the East was of secondary importance, an assumption which few historians today would accept.

The series never became the modern counterpart of Migne's *Patrologia* or the *Ante-Nicene Fathers* as Case had hoped. The very fact that he had frequently compared the series to these classics of early Christian literature revealed several misconceptions which may have been common among the Chicago sponsors of and participants in the sources project. The comparison implied, first, that there was no substantial difference between the nature of the historical sources in the patristic and modern periods. Such a view ignored the fact that the selection process required for the publication of patristic documents was largely a matter of finding and authenticating what few documents had been preserved, whereas the sheer volume of available data concerning modern history necessitated the use of discriminatory principles which would reduce it to a manageable size. This fact alone made it impossible that any single collection of sources would ever sustain as comprehensive a relation to a knowledge of American religion as Migne's collection sustained to a knowledge of early Christianity. The fact that the project was conceived not by trained specialists in American history but rather by historians of early Christianity (Mathews and Case) goes a long way toward explaining the incongruities of Case's comparison.

A second and more subtle implication of the comparison was the suggestion that documents tracing the frontier history of obscure Baptist, Methodist, Presbyterian, and Congregationalist pioneers might one day be as important to historians of Christianity as the works of Ignatius, Irenaeus, or Augustine. Behind such a suggestion lay the concept, characteristic of Mathews and Case, that a glorious new future lay ahead of mankind, a future of spiritual and moral progress of which American Protestantism was the vanguard and the Divinity School of the University of Chicago the herald.

THE SWEET SYNTHESIS

The same assumptions which limited the American sources project to data concerning the frontier history of four Protestant denominations also determined the shape of Sweet's synthesis of American religious history as it emerged in his numerous books and articles. The basic characteristics of that synthesis, as we have seen, were first articulated by Sweet in the publications of the DePauw years. The synthesis took an increasingly standard form in the works written after he went to Chicago, for once Sweet had mentally constructed his synthesis, he never made any significant changes in it. The single passage in all of Sweet's works which comes closest to describing his central thesis states,

> . . . it was the success with which the several religious bodies functioned in the middle west that was to determine which of the American Churches were to be large and evenly distributed throughout the nation, and which of the Churches were to be typically American. The eastern Churches which failed to make a major impact upon the middle west tended to remain small and sectional.[63]

Thus Sweet was interested primarily in chronicling the growth of successful churches, churches whose large size and national distribution determined for him their "typically American" status.

This desire to explain institutional growth followed the tradition of another Methodist historian, Daniel Dorchester, who wrote in the late nineteenth century.[64] Dorchester assumed that true religions spread fastest, that the basic task of the church was to maximize expansion, and that the strength and influence of a denomination were best measured in membership statistics. Sweet shared these assumptions.

At the heart of Sweet's thesis lay the conviction that the first great wave of westward expansion, which took place during the two generations after the Revolution in the Mississippi Valley, determined the subsequent shape of American religion. The territory into which the churches were expanding was an uncivilized frontier which rendered many elements of established eastern religion counterproductive or obsolete. The frontier functioned as a kind of Darwinian testing-ground in which churches with old world, vestigial encumbrances declined or died, whereas the younger, vigorous churches more fit for frontier life survived and prospered. In Sweet's words, "the churches which devised the best methods for following the population as it pushed westward were the ones destined to become the great American churches."[65] As we shall see, the successful methods included, first, a strong, centralized denominational organization capable of planning, coordinating, and executing westward expansion, and second, the use of revivalism as a technique to reach the mass of unchurched settlers.

The impression conveyed by the thesis passage quoted above is that size and national distribution were the sole criteria for determining Sweet's "typically American" churches. Such an impression, however, is misleading, for Sweet was unwilling to consider two very large and well-distributed groups, Roman Catholics and Lutherans, as "typically American." This omission alone reveals that other, more hidden assumptions were operative in Sweet's thinking concerning American history. These assumptions were characteristic not only of Sweet's childhood world in frontier Kansas but also of the entire Protestant American tradition of religious historiography before him. A detailed examination of Sweet's treatment of those churches he considered of major importance brings these hidden assumptions into better focus.

The denomination which dominated Sweet's attention was of course his own Methodist church. Since he had virtually immersed himself in Methodist sources since his graduate training, it is not surprising that his understanding of Methodist history informed and shaped his general synthesis. From the beginning, in his formative DePauw works, he ascribed Methodism's success to an ingenious polity perfectly suited to frontier conditions. This conviction continued throughout his career. "More than any other single factor," he claimed, " 'itineracy' was responsible for the rapid spread of Methodism throughout the United States in the frontier period."[66] The itinerant system of Methodism was built around the circuit rider who could serve not merely one but rather five to ten small, scattered churches. The system also included a very authoritarian administrative structure: "The Methodist system was highly centralized, with the power of sending the circuit riders to their circuits wholly in the hands of the superintendents."[67] This organization was for Sweet the key to Methodist expansion. When he pointed out in his major synthetic work that "the first American religious body to form a national organization was the Methodists,"[68] he was implying that their priority in that respect would prove to be a contributing factor in their subsequent growth and success.

A secondary factor in Methodist frontier growth was its theology, which Sweet described in *The Story of Religions in America* in a passage practically lifted from one of his earlier DePauw works:

The doctrine preached by the Methodist circuit riders was also well adapted to meet the hearty acceptance of the frontiersmen. It was a gospel of free will and free grace, as opposed to the doctrines of limited grace and predestination preached by the Calvinistic Presbyterians, or even the milder Calvinism of the Baptists. The frontier Methodist preachers brought home to the pioneers the fact that they were the masters of their own destiny, an emphasis which fitted in exactly with the new democracy rising in the West, for both emphasized the actual equality among all men.[69]

This Arminian theology led to the development of a new kind of revivalism of which the Methodists were the most vigorous advocates. The older,

Presbyterian-Congregational type of revivalism of the first half of the eighteenth century made only a limited appeal. It was a type of revivalism which was based on Calvinistic doctrines; the kind of revivalism which swept the frontier was Arminian, in emphasis. The first offered salvation to the few; the second offered it to all. The former was aristocratic; the latter democratic.[70]

The later revivalism was more effective in motivating and rendering "less sodden the great unleavened masses of men."[71] Thus, "as a frontier religious force the Methodists were undoubtedly the most successful, if success be judged by the numbers that were reached by the Methodist gospel."[72]

Sweet's treatment of Baptists, the second denomination in his Protestant coalition, appears at first glance to support his general theses. Baptists successfully met the challenge of the frontier through the use of revivalism. Their frontier growth made them a truly national church. But the Baptist resemblance to Methodism disappears quickly when a closer look reveals basic contrasts between these two most successful frontier denominations. The problem here is that the Baptists had neither the centralized organization nor the Arminian theology of the Methodists. Thus, if Sweet's explanation of Methodist growth is correct, Baptists should have done far worse than Methodists on the frontier instead of doing almost as well. Sweet at first did not seem to recognize this difficulty. Instead, trying to be consistent, he attempted to explain Baptist growth by reference to their church associations: "It was only through the combining of the strength of these little churches, . . . through associational organization, that the Baptists became an effective instrument in meeting frontier needs."[73] This attempt to link Baptist success with central organization was ultimately unconvincing in view of Sweet's own admission that extra-congregational organizations, antithetical to Baptist primitivism, were strongly eschewed by most frontier Baptists.[74]

Later in his career Sweet abandoned his attempt to explain Baptist growth in terms of central organization. As an alternative, he suggested,

The phenomenal growth of the Baptist denomination in the United States has been due to four main factors: first, the simplicity of its doctrine; second, the democracy of its organization; third, its ability to propagate itself *without overhead machinery*; and fourth, its appeal to the common man because of its simple doctrine and its democratic polity. Or to put it in another way, the Baptists found in America, and especially in frontier America, a soil suited to its particular genius [italics mine].[75]

Sweet was sensitive to the fact that the Baptist success, which occurred primarily in the South, did not square with his general theses explaining frontier church growth. During his second year at Chicago, he did comment to Herbert Gambrell, a graduate student, "that the Southern Baptists mystified him and he hoped someday to spend time in the southern Bible Belt to see what 'made them tick.'" After his southern retirement began, he admitted to the same man, "They still amaze me. They do the impossible—they achieve unanimity without any organization whatsoever. That doesn't make sense, but it seems to work."[76]

What ultimately bound the Baptists and the Methodists together for Sweet, in spite of their incongruences, was their phenomenal frontier growth. He finally attributed this common success to the universal appeal made by the Baptist and Methodist revivalists. The Presbyterian, Congregational, and Lutheran ministers, on the one hand, were often directed toward a single class or nationality group.

The Methodists and Baptists, on the other hand, went forth in the western wilderness to win people of all kinds to the Christian way of life. Neither felt any special commitment to any one class or group but thought in terms of western society as a whole. This one fact helps to account for the wide distribution of these two bodies throughout the nation today.[77]

In contrast to the Methodist and Baptist success, the groups third and fourth in importance in Sweet's Protestant coalition, the Presbyterians and Congregationalists, were hampered from the beginning of western migration by a church polity which was suited only to a settled and civilized environment. Sweet noted that in the post-Revolutionary period,

> The Presbyterians had the best chance . . . of becoming the greatest of all the American churches both in point of numbers and in influence. . . . Already their presbyteries, their churches and their ministers were to be found farthest west, and their leaders were imbued with the sturdy spirit of the pioneers. One of the purposes of this volume is to show, through the documents illustrating the *methods* of Presbyterians, why they failed to take full advantage of their frontier opportunities [italics mine].[78]

The chief problems in frontier Presbyterianism were that

The average Presbyterian clergyman ministered as a rule to not more than three churches, and usually to but two . . . and ministers were not settled until there were enough Presbyterian members in a given community to provide for his support. Then too the Presbyterians were a particularly rigid body in both doctrine and polity, and every innovation to meet the particular needs or problems of a new country was always strongly opposed.[79]

It was primarily the polity, then, of Presbyterianism which limited its success on the frontier.

Likewise, Congregationalism was hindered by its organizational structures, which "were devised for a homogeneous population and for a 'narrow home use' and were, therefore, not adapted to aggressive action on a national scale."[80] A more serious weakness was "its lack of any centralized authority,"[81] a result of its failure to unite effectively after the Revolution.[82] Another serious indictment against Congregationalism was its elitism, a characteristic which made it altogether incompatible with the egalitarian common man of the frontier. Sweet lamented,

A dynamic and aggressive Congregationalism in the middle west would have helped to put new life into the self-satisfied, upper-classish Congregationalism of New England; as it was, New England Congregationalism dominated the Church throughout these crucial years to its hurt. Congregationalism did not spring out of the frontier soil, but was a hundred per cent transplanted body.[83]

In summary, Sweet's description of frontier Protestantism is dominated by accounts of institutional success and failure. In each of the four denominations which occupy his attention, numerical growth is primarily explained by church polity, including organization, evangelistic techniques, and general compatibility with frontier conditions, and second, by theology. Factors unique to religious institutions such as the motivating power of religious experience itself were, with a few notable exceptions,[84] largely ignored. The distinctions in polity which Sweet ingeniously drew between the major frontier denominations are best illustrated in an often quoted passage from his *Story of Religions in America*:

In a new region where there were no congregations, the method the Presbyterians adopted in forming new congregations was a slow and often painful process. Two or three congregations generally had to unite to call a minister, and this caused still further delay. On the other hand the Methodist circuit rider was not called but was sent to the people to form classes and churches, while the Baptist farmer-preacher was one of the people and moved out with the settlers. Or to put it concisely, the Presbyterian preacher was called; the Methodist preacher was sent; the Baptist preacher simply came with the people.[85]

Sweet's articulation of the causes of church growth, while it fails to account entirely for the whole of frontier Protestantism, especially in the case of the Baptists, nevertheless stands as a legitimate treatment of the relationship between church polity and church growth, and between institutional ideology and institutional success. Few historians would question the assertion that an institution's organization and ideals significantly affect its popular appeal.

The method in which Sweet presented the foregoing synthesis of American religion combined two rather disparate approaches to the writing of history. The first approach, a consequence of his graduate training under advocates of scientific history, involved the use of great masses of empirical data—names, dates, places, statistics—the significance of which was often left to the reader to determine. Thus the nineteenth-century assumption that accumulated data organized chronologically constituted history occasionally produced statements such as this one: "In 1720, Virginia contained twenty-nine counties and forty-four parishes, large and small."[86] Since Sweet does not utilize these figures in comparisons with other years or other states, their importance remains hidden from the reader. Unlike the archivist historians who venerated this method, however, Sweet was also willing to suggest broad interpretive theses which dealt with the particular significance of the historical data presented. The preoccupation with naked, empirical data combined somewhat incongruously with the use of interpretive theses was what Sidney Mead meant in stating that "Professor Sweet has always worn a Turner mantle rather lightly over a McMaster frame."[87] The results of such a method were reflected in typical chapters of his synthetic works. The opening paragraphs were usually broadly interpretive, describing general historical trends, but they were followed by a tremendous bulk of data organized solely along denominational and chronological lines.[88]

The basic flaw in Sweet's synthesis was what it omitted. If his works could be viewed as studies of the major British-derived, Protestant denominations on the midwestern frontier, then they would stand in need of much less criticism. But the titles of his general works reflected his own conviction that he was telling a larger story —the story of *religion* in *America*.[89] It must be admitted that Sweet did not limit all his interpretive generalizations to the early nineteenth-century frontier. In an article which was the basis for his inaugural lecture at Chicago, he described four factors significant for American church history, of which the frontier was only one. The others were the influence of religious radicals, the parallels between American political and church history, and the issue of slavery.[90] Yet the theme which he traced firmly centered on the growth of frontier churches as the primary explanation for the ultimate shape of American religion. This focus meant that important post–Civil War developments such as the growth of immigrant churches and urban religion would not be emphasized.

But even if Sweet's frontier focus, with its geographical and temporal limitations, could be accepted as valid, it would not adequately explain why he omitted from positive consideration two very large churches with definite frontier histories, the Catholic and the Lutheran. Nor would it explain his disproportionate attention to Congregationalism, which was far stronger in New England than on the frontier; nor his uniform disparagement of sectarian groups whether they flourished on the frontier, as did Mormonism, or in the East, as did Christian Science.

Sweet's negative evaluation of Roman Catholicism affected, for example, his treatment of Catholic Indian missions. After eulogizing the feeble Methodist and Presbyterian efforts among the Indians of the Pacific Northwest, he tersely admitted, "The Catholics were more successful in their Indian work than were the Protestants and it is claimed that in six years six thousand Indians had embraced the Catholic faith."[91] If these statistics had reflected a Methodist triumph, it is likely that the words "it is claimed" would have been omitted and "Catholic faith" would have unambiguously become "Christian faith." Very rarely did Sweet refer to Catholics simply as "Christian" without qualification. He patronized the phenomenal success of Spanish colonial missionaries by noting that "thousands of natives had been brought to at least a nominal acceptance of Christianity."[92] In spite of this acknowledgment, he somehow managed to state, quite falsely, that "the Congregationalists have the longest record of missionary endeavor of any of the American churches."[93]

The most explicit account of Sweet's view of American Catholicism was written in *The American Churches*, a series of lectures given before a British audience in 1946. Here Sweet described Catholicism as an aristocratic vestige of medieval Europe inimical to America. He stated that "a great majority of the American people still look upon the Roman Catholic Church as a foreign transplantation, that has never been acclimatized to the American political and cultural soil, and the general assumption is that it never will nor can become so."[94] Sweet clearly was among this great majority. So was his colleague at Chicago, W. E. Garrison, whom he quoted with approval: "No more serious error can be made in judging of the spirit, the attitudes, and the methods of Roman Catholicism in the United States at the present time than the assumption that it has been permeated and transformed in some subtle fashion by the spirit of American institutions."[95] Sweet's final verdict was that Catholicism posed a serious threat to American ideals because "the Roman Catholic hierarchy are aiming at a kind of world domination, inimical to the basic freedom of all our freedoms, religious liberty."[96]

Other groups for which Sweet found no important role in his historical synthesis included the Lutheran bodies, whose influence he viewed as "the least important" of all the European churches,[97] primarily because most Lutherans were Scandinavian or German and their inability to speak English, he claimed, segregated them from American life. He grouped Lutheranism with Catholicism as religious movements which were essentially unaffected by the American environment. In discussing frontier religion he admitted,

I am, of course, leaving out of account the Roman Catholic and the newer Lutheran churches which arose as a result of nineteenth-century immigration because neither were important factors during the early years of the last century. Both were to a large degree direct European transplantations, and neither was modified in any marked degree by frontier influence.[98]

Thus Lutherans were considered as mere Old World transplantations and were summarily dismissed from serious consideration as an American church. Sweet likewise asserted that the black churches had made "no notable contribution to the religious life of America."[99]

If Sweet's narrow focus on a supposed coalition of three or four Protestant denominations caused him to ignore several major religious groups, it totally eliminated any careful attention to smaller sectarian groups. In this respect his history was but one step improved over those denominational histories whose confined scope he repudiated.[100] His outlook was broader in that he included in his purview more than a single denomination. Yet his glancing attention to the few small sects which he mentioned displayed as patronizing an attitude toward them as ever a denominational historian displayed toward rival groups:

Many of these strange religious movements were the unhealthy offspring of the revivals of the [eighteen-] thirties, forties, and fifties. But along with the rise of Mormonism, Adventism, Perfectionism and all the other "isms," the great Protestant churches were adding tens of thousands of sane Christians to their membership . . .[101]

A "strange" movement was thus for Sweet usually an "unhealthy" movement. He was truly uncomfortable with sectarian groups whose theology lay outside the bounds of his Protestant coalition, groups such as Mormons, Adventists, Christian Scientists, Shakers, Spiritualists, and the like—a serious problem for a historian of American religion. He mentioned Mary Baker Eddy, for example, only to refer to "the absurdity of her 'philosophic sophistries.' "[102] He constructed a terribly misinformed description, almost a caricature, of the *Book of Mormon*, followed with the predictable conclusion: "Mormonism has persisted and has grown immeasurably strong in spite of its crudity and bizarre origin because of its effective, highly centralized organization, and the stress it places upon the simple frontier virtues."[103] One of Sweet's Mormon doctoral students pleaded with him to change the tone of some of these passages, but Sweet refused.[104]

Sweet's puzzlement at the growth of sectarian groups illustrates his failure to recognize the quality of religious experience engendered by a movement as a crucial motivating factor in its growth, a curious flaw for a Methodist historian of religion. Perhaps as a result of his avowedly secular and "scientific" approach, his explanations of church growth were based on criteria which could apply just as well to political and social organizations as to explicitly religious institutions. Such an approach rendered his treatment of sects singularly unpenetrating. They were treated as little more than institutional and theological anomalies.

Among the minority groups, the most offensive to Sweet were those characterized by ecstasy or revelation, groups to which he routinely applied the term "fanatic." It is true that his veneration of revivalism was accompanied by a theoretical defense of the emotional element in religion. He even asserted, "In certain realms of life emotion is a better guide than reason. And that is true in the higher realms more frequently than in the lower." But he significantly added, "And yet over-emotionalized religion deserves all that can be said in condemnation."[105] "Over-emotionalized" religion certainly included for Sweet much of the wilder phenomena of the frontier camp meetings in which Methodists took an active part. Sweet was profoundly embarrassed by such activities, and his view of revivalism consequently suffered. One of his most defensive statements concerning Methodism occurred on this point:

It has been stated that the Methodist preachers desired to work the people up to a state of religious frenzy and that they took special delight in the "jerks" and the "holy laugh" and encouraged trances and visions. But nothing could be farther from the truth. There were few if any fanatics among the responsible Methodist leaders. . . .[106]

A clue to Sweet's view of the cause of religious "fanaticism" appeared in his discussion of upstate New York's "burned-over district":

These counties had been settled by New Englanders, the first wave being of "rather unsavory fame," though they were followed by an intelligent and industrious class from eastern New York and New England. The mingling of these two classes gave a peculiar psychological character to the people, producing, on the one hand, sane and progressive social movements, and, on the other, tendencies toward fanaticism.[107]

Presumably Sweet was implying that the "unsavory" class produced the "fanaticism," while the "intelligent and industrious" class produced the "sane and progressive social movements." This view of "fanaticism" as a class phenomenon was based on a highly conjectural construction of frontier psychology in which, according to Sweet, frontier illiteracy and ignorance issued in "the extravagant type of revivalism."[108] Thus, in Sweet's view, no educated, civilized person could ever engage in religious "fanaticism." Perhaps Sweet's attitude reflected the fact that Methodist piety had cooled somewhat from its frontier state by Sweet's day. Methodist revivals still occurred, but they were calm and respectable affairs held in brick buildings by educated ministers, most of whom would have been as uncomfortable as Sweet at the most uninhibited events of the early Methodist camp meetings.

Sweet did throw one bone to the sects. Although he often described some of them—Spiritualists, Adventists, and Shakers, for example—in a way that made them seem so irrational or bizarre as to be socially dysfunctional,[109] he realized later in his career that the thriving existence of such a great number of sectarian groups on American soil pointed to a very different conclusion: "The very fact that they have increased so rapidly is an indication that they occupy a necessary place among the religious organizations of our day, and are supplying needs and reaching people which at present seem to be beyond the power of the 'enlightened' Churches to supply or reach."[110] In spite of this admission, however, Sweet never took seriously either the number or the nature of such groups in his general treatment of American religion.

Sweet's portrait of "typically American" religion, then, excluded from serious consideration the Roman Catholic, Lutheran, and black churches, as well as the multitude of sectarian groups. A simple look at the space devoted to these groups in his most popular synthetic work, *The Story of Religions in America*, illustrates his view of their relative importance. As the following charts show (pp. 88, 89), Sweet devoted more attention to his four-denomination Protestant coalition than to all other single groups combined. The Roman Catholic church, though by the end of the nineteenth century almost as large as the combined membership of Sweet's Protestant coalition, was given only one-seventh as much space as the coalition. Black churches were given only four pages and Judaism only one page. While there is much that these statistics do not reveal about the finer points of Sweet's emphasis, they are indicative of the general shape of his view of American religion.

When his historical construction of American religion is measured against the interpretive principles which he explicitly set down, it is clear that the principles do not adequately account for what Sweet chose to stress and what he chose to ignore. As we have seen, Sweet claimed that his criteria for selecting four large denomi-

CHAPTERS 1-12 (to 1780) | CHAPTERS 13-21 (after 1780)

PAGES 60   40   20   0   20   40   60   80   100   120 PAGES

General Information (No single denomination or group discussed)

61   121¼

58 Puritan-Congregational   2¾

28 Presbyterian   29

21 Baptist   16

4 Methodist 18

25 Anglican-Episcopal   11½

15 Roman Catholic   10

11 Lutheran   5

15 Dutch Reformed   ¼

14 Quakers   ¼

9 Moravians   ¼

Disciples   7

4 German Reformed   1½

Mormon 5

8 Others   17½

PAGES

Communal Groups   4½
Black Churches   4
Dunkers   3
Mennonites   3
Millerites   3
Schwenkfelders   2
United Brethren   1½
Christian Scientists   1½
Jewish Bodies   1
Spiritualists   1
Shakers   ½
Evangelical Church   ¼
Pentecostal (Holiness) ¼

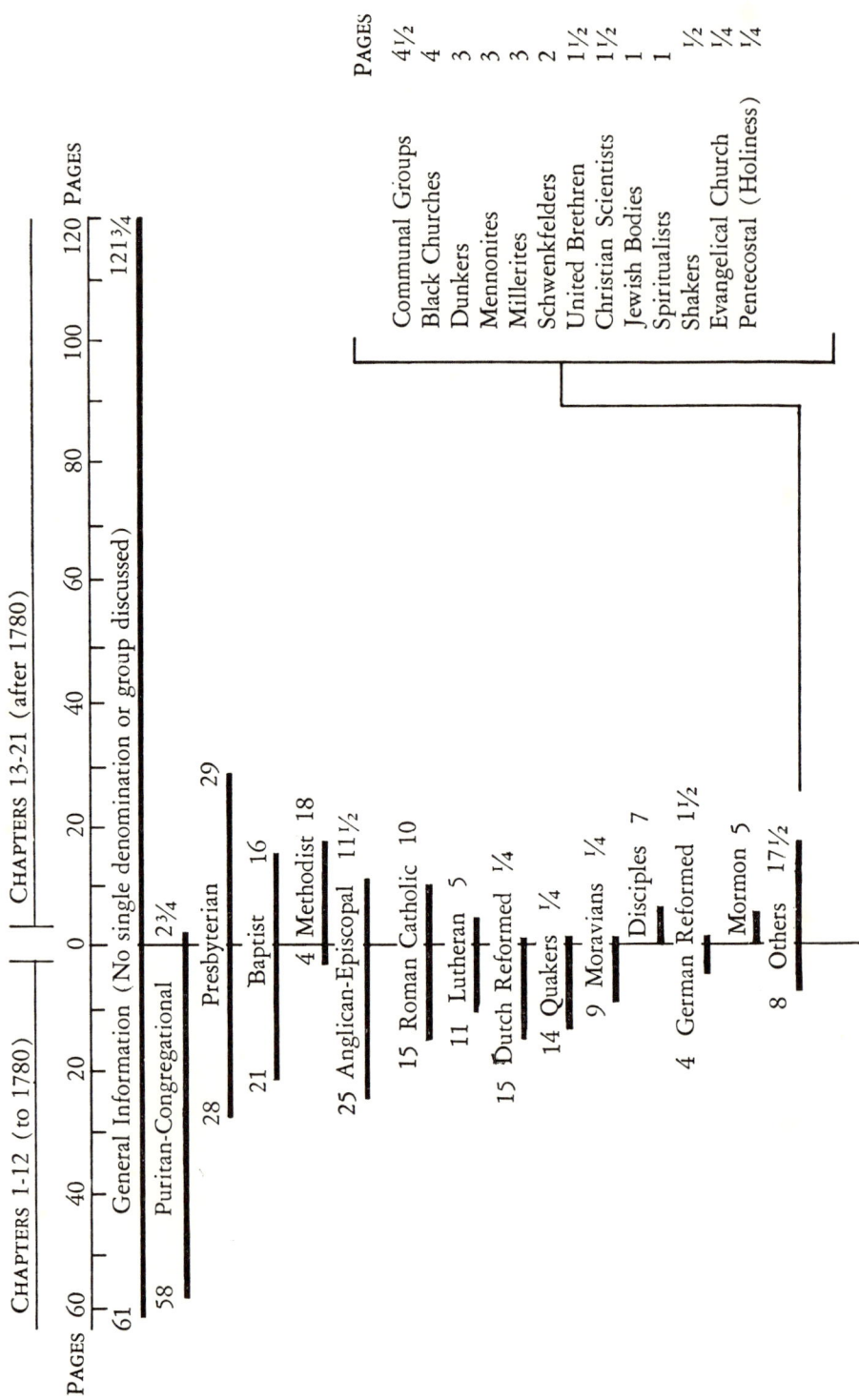

FIG. 2. Space devoted to specific denominations in William Warren Sweet's *The Story of Religions in America*, 1st ed.

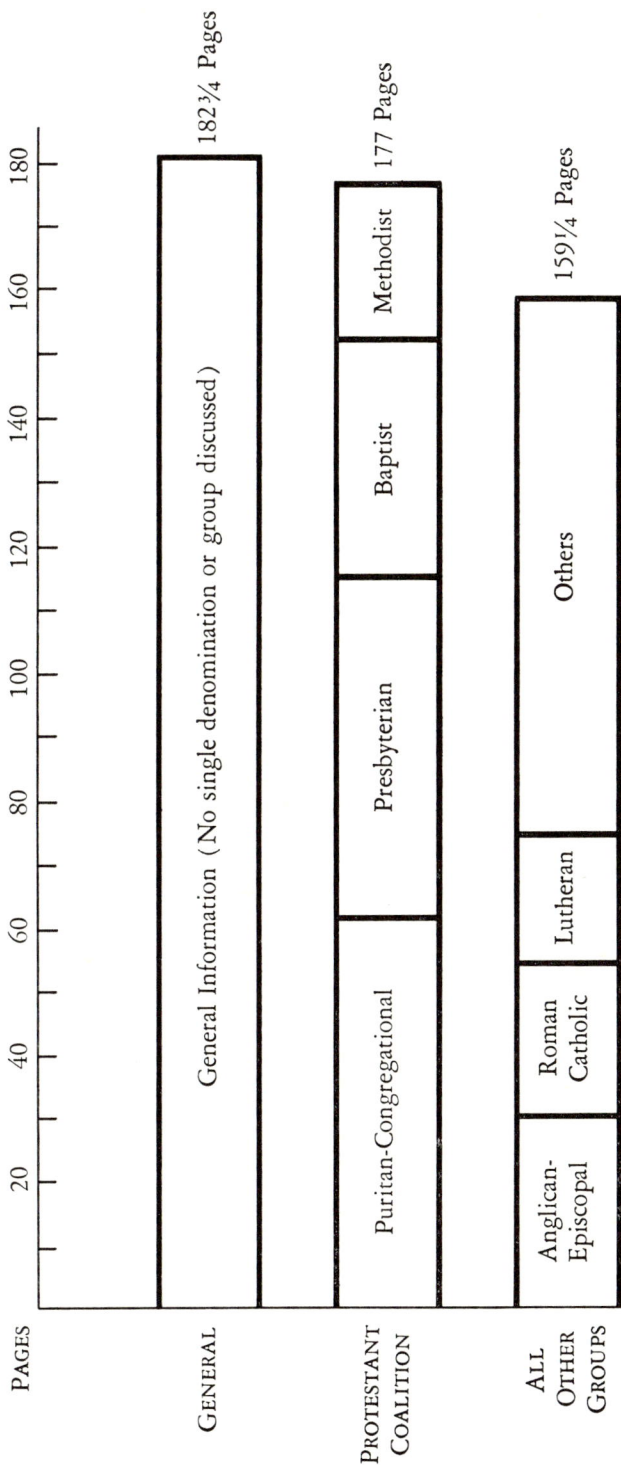

FIG. 3. Space devoted to groups of denominations in William Warren Sweet's *The Story of Religions in America*, 1st ed.

nations as "typically American" and "most influential" were size and
national distribution—simple, straightforward matters of statistics and
demography. As we have also seen, however, his list of "typically
American" churches omits two major groups which, by the same sta-
tistical and demographic considerations, surely ought to be included.
This fact reveals that not all of Sweet's interpretive principles were
explicit in his works. Clearly there were unstated values and assumptions guiding his approach to his subject.

Sweet's view of what was and what was not a "typically American"
church ultimately had its roots in the Protestant vision of social
reality with which he grew up in frontier Kansas and from which he
never departed. In that setting most Catholics were relatively recent
immigrants whose poverty, ethnic allegiances, and religious practices
tended to restrict them from full participation in surrounding society.
Lutherans not only were a tiny minority, but also had a high proportion of non-English-speaking members which isolated them from
society in general. The small communities of sectarian groups that
existed—mostly Mormons, Moravians, and Mennonites—were strictly
segregated from the majority of Kansans, usually in colonized towns
founded by sectarian leaders as havens for their followers. Clearly
these groups were not active participants in the prevailing community ideology, a fact which made full social inclusion impossible. We
have seen in an earlier chapter that that ideology, so well epitomized
by Baldwin, Kansas, centered in the values of revivalistic Protestantism advocated by a cooperative Protestant coalition. An important
part of the Methodist childhood world of William Warren Sweet,
this coalition effectively consisted of the same denominations which
later dominated his construction of American religious history.

Sweet was certainly not alone in his assumptions concerning social
reality. Similar assumptions were characteristic of virtually all of
his predecessors who wrote general histories of American religion.
Robert Baird, a Presbyterian, composed the first such work in 1844
for a European audience. He divided American denominations into
"evangelical" and "non-evangelical" categories, the former including
all bodies which accepted "the great doctrines which are universally
conceded by Protestants to be fundamental and necessary to salvation,"
and the latter those which did not.[111] Among the "evangelical" groups,

Baird listed all large Protestant denominations. Among the "non-evangelical" were Roman Catholics ("the sect that has buried the Truth amid a heap of corruptions of heathenish origin"),[112] Jews, and selected sectarian bodies, including Mormonism ("the grossest of all the delusions that Satanic malignity or human ambition ever sought to propagate").[113] For Baird, the religion which characterized the American people was without question "evangelical" Christianity.[114]

Some forty years later (1888), a Methodist minister, Daniel Dorchester, published his massive history. Dorchester retained Baird's category of "evangelical Protestant" groups which he regarded as "the chief molding religious force of the country."[115] He added Roman Catholicism as a separate category, optimistically claiming that in America "Romanism has already lost much of her hideous character."[116] A third category, "divergent groups," included the sects, of which Mormonism was described in a mixed metaphor as having a "beastly, defiant head" and as being a "local ulcer."[117]

The work of the Congregationalist Leonard W. Bacon, published in 1901 as the synthetic volume of the American Church History Series, contained no explicit categories similar to Baird's or Dorchester's, yet the same concepts were present. Bacon was more polite toward Catholics, but in discussing the "acclimatization of the Catholic Church in America" he looked forward to the rise of leaders more "in sympathy with the ruling ideas of the country and the age."[118] His work was united by no clear thesis, but he focused on Protestant developments and viewed sectarian groups in much the same terms as his predecessors. Mormonism, for example, was characterized as "a system of gross, palpable imposture contrived by a disreputable adventurer."[119] It was "only incidentally . . . connected with the history of American Christianity,"[120] whereas a group such as Presbyterianism was described in the early nineteenth century as "unmistakably" representing "the Christian citizenship of the whole country."[121]

Henry K. Rowe, a student of J. Franklin Jameson and professor at Newton Seminary, published a synthetic work in 1924 entitled *The History of Religion in the United States*. Focusing on the democratizing effect of the American environment, he traced the institutional and theological "emancipation" of Old World churches in a New World setting. Like Sweet, he spoke of a body of "democratic"

churches "true to the spirit of America"; for him, this category included Methodists, Baptists, Congregationalists, Disciples, and even
Episcopalians.[122] Like Sweet, Rowe refused to count Lutherans among
the "distinctly American denominations."[123] Similarly, the Catholic
church was excluded because it "suffers continually from its lack of
kinship with the spirit of freedom and democracy. Its genius is European, not American."[124] Consequently, he found it "strange that
Catholicism flourishes in America."[125] Like Sweet, Rowe patronized
sectarian groups as religious aberrations. Mormonism, for example,
was described as "an immoral propaganda," "an alien religion based
upon a fraud," and "an ambitious state within a state."[126] In spite of
the general title of his work, he devoted no more than a paragraph to
Judaism. Black churches also received only a paragraph, including
the statement that "too often negro church members were guilty of
moral lapses."[127]

It is clear that Sweet's concept of essential American religion
stood well within the historiographical tradition formed by his predecessors, all Protestants like himself. For those who wrote within
this tradition, the status of a denomination was determined not by
empirical criteria of size or demography, but rather by whether the
denomination lay within the bounds of the ideological "mainstream"
of which they themselves were a part. What then were the criteria
for inclusion in "mainstream" American religion?

Martin E. Marty, in an unpublished study of general histories of
American religion from Baird to the mid-twentieth century, has
identified six factors which seemed to accord favorable status to denominations in the twelve works which he considered. These factors
were (1) Anglo-Saxon or Scotch-Irish derivation, (2) New England
beginnings, (3) social prestige, and (4) a Protestant heritage, plus
the more important characteristics of being positively related to (5)
the establishment of religious liberty and (6) westward expansion.[128]
While few denominations could meet all six criteria, any which met
five of them could be sure of inclusion as a "mainstream" denomination, or in Sweet's terms, as a "typically American" denomination.
Marty concluded his study with the suggestion that the ultimate assumption behind the concept of the mainstream as it appeared in these
histories was that the American environment was itself redemptive.[129]

The criteria for mainstream American religion outlined by Marty, coupled with the assumption about the American environment, surely were operative in Sweet's case. Baptist churches meet all the criteria except perhaps the third; Methodism and Presbyterianism can be seen as meeting all but the second; and Congregationalism all but the fifth. Lutherans fail on points one and two; Catholics on one and four; Episcopalians on five and six. The assumption that the New World environment was redemptive was implicit in Sweet's theme: the challenges, opportunities, and restrictions of the frontier underlay the success of those better and more progressive denominations which eventually became known as "typically American."

The idea of a Protestant mainstream was of course an integral part of the mental universe of influential American leaders, particularly during the late nineteenth and early twentieth centuries when the rural Protestant establishment was being overwhelmed by immigrants with very different social and religious ideologies. In the face of this threat, Protestants became more assertive and defensive, a fact which can be seen in the popular idea of Manifest Destiny, in the Progressive Movement, in the Immigration Restriction League, in Prohibition, and in the Protestant political, social, and moral order which they all presupposed.[130] Thus Sweet's version of American religious history which excluded broad segments of the religious spectrum was one of many expressions of a Protestant establishment view of history. The distinguishing marks of Sweet's construction were the result of insights peculiar to his own Kansas background. His emphasis on Methodist growth as paradigmatic, his veneration of the midwestern frontier, and his intense respect for the personal sacrifice and devotion which the rugged frontier made necessary in a pioneer religious leader—these elements brought to Sweet's works a spirit and focus which were absent in the histories of his eastern predecessors. At the same time, the fact that Sweet was representative of a historiographical tradition makes him and his frontier background more significant than either may warrant in themselves. Both Sweet and Baldwin epitomized an important segment of American history.

RISING ACADEMIC STATUS

The work which was most responsible for popularizing Sweet's synthesis of American religious history was his *The Story of Religions in America*, a work which he began contemplating as soon as he arrived at the University of Chicago.[131] Sweet always arranged his courses so that they would prepare him for whatever writing he faced. He therefore inserted into the curriculum shortly after his arrival a course entitled

The Great Democratic Churches of America.—This course will emphasize the history of the three churches which seem to have had the largest appeal and influence in American life—the Baptist, Methodist and Presbyterian. Beginning with their European background the course will trace these churches through their establishment and national origin in America; it will discuss their differences in doctrinal emphasis and polity, and will attempt to appraise their peculiar contributions to American life.[132]

Material initially collected as lectures for this course became the basis for *The Story of Religions in America.*

Sweet's narrative and synthetic skills were the basis for the extraordinary readability of the book. His ability to tell a story well has been mentioned in an earlier chapter. His wide experience as a preacher no doubt increased that ability. On an Atlantic crossing in the summer of 1931, for example, Sweet was asked to preach at a Sunday worship service. He told a story of a boy lost in the woods at night, not knowing where to turn until finally he heard his father's voice calling him. One of his hearers later wrote him and offered this description of the powerful impact of the story: "I remember so well the Captain of the Boat and how the tears ran down his face as you were preaching."[133]

The talent for synthesis which Sweet possessed was widely recognized when he won first prize in a 1930 contest sponsored by the *Chicago Tribune* for the best 500-word history of the United States. The contest attracted 3,759 entries, including many by well-known historians. Sweet's essay was a masterpiece of selectivity and economy, dashed off while traveling by train, in response to his wife's suggestion that he enter.[134] The essay emphasized the importance of the western frontier as the setting for "a new type of democracy," and did not mention religion at all.[135] The contest carried an award of $1,000, which Sweet invested in a Sixty-third Street bank, only to lose it when the bank failed the following year.[136]

In the winter of 1928, Sweet began negotiating with Harper and Brothers to publish his then unwritten manuscript. His editor, Eugene Exman, concerned with prospective sales, urged him to do a "popular treatment" rather than a "technical and factual history of the American church." He wrote Sweet,

The time has come for the American people generally to be made conscious of the importance of the church in the development of the country. The man who gives that interpretation and gives it well, will not only have made a name for himself in the literature of our generation, but will also have made a distinct contribution to the present-day efficacy of the church.[137]

As the work progressed, Exman urged Sweet to include material dealing with Catholicism and Judaism, unless he wanted to change the title to reflect an exclusive focus on Protestantism.[138] Sweet replied suggesting his own reason for including Catholicism: "I feel that the Catholics cannot very well be left out, since their presence in America has undoubtedly influenced American Protestantism, and certain movements cannot be explained without some understanding of their place in American history. The Jews might be summarized in a rather brief space."[139]

The book wwent to the printer in the late spring of 1930. Exman wrote Sweet that in view of his winning the *Tribune* contest, perhaps he was best qualified to write the publicity synopsis of the forthcoming book.[140] Sweet complied, composing a paragraph which illustrated the kind of impression he wanted the book to make, namely, the impression of an interpretive history which placed religious developments in a broad cultural context:

The United States presents a more complicated religious pattern than exists among any other people in the world, for according to the most recent religious census there are two hundred and thirteen denominations of Christians in America. What are the forces which have been responsible for such confusion? Is there a common thread which runs through the three hundred years of our religious history which binds these divergent elements into a whole? *The Story of Religions in America* not only discusses the religious forces, but relates these to the political,

economic, and social factors which were operating at the same time in
American life. Equally important for an understanding of this phase of
American history and life, the author has found the magic strand which
brings understanding out of seeming confusion.[141]

When the book appeared it was quickly acclaimed as the best
historical treatment of American religion. W. M. Gewehr's review
in the *American Historical Review* was representative. It stated that
no writer was "more familiar with what Professor Jameson has called
the American *Acta Sanctorum* than Professor Sweet," pronounced
the work "the best single volume on the subject," and predicted "a
wide acceptance." The single observation about the work which appeared repeatedly in the dozens of reviews it received was that it was
remarkably free of religious bias. Gewehr stated that the book was
"written from an impartial and unsectarian point of view."[142] The
virtual unanimity of reviewers on this point illustrates how firmly
entrenched and unquestioned the concept of Protestant hegemony was
in 1930. That the concept was shared by Sweet's colleagues in the
church history department is clear from W. E. Garrison's review,
which asserted that Professor Sweet embraced "the point of view and
the method of the scientific historian. He has nothing to prove and
no denominational ideas to sell."[143]

The Story of Religions in America became a popular text for the
growing number of courses in American religious history being offered
in colleges and seminaries throughout the country, an increasing number of which were being taught by Sweet's own students. The book
sold well in its first edition, averaging about five hundred copies per
year during the 1930s. A second edition, published in 1939, had average yearly sales during the 1940s of over one thousand. A third edition was published in 1950, containing additional chapters which
brought the narrative to the mid-twentieth century. Its yearly sales
averaged almost three thousand during the 1950s and gradually declined during the 1960s from twenty-five hundred in 1960 to seven
hundred in 1970. In 1973 the publication rights were purchased by
Baker Book House, which still offers the book in paperback. By that
time, its total sales had exceeded forty thousand.[144] The fact that the
work has now been published for over fifty years and is still being

sold is itself ample testimony both to Sweet's skill as a synthesist and
to the continuation of the ideology of Protestant hegemony in certain
segments of American society.

Eugene Exman was right in telling Sweet that the person who
constructed a popular interpretive history of American religion would
make a name for himself. It was in no small part owing to the success of his general history that Sweet's reputation soared during the
early 1930s. He was invited to serve as visiting professor of Church
History at his alma mater, Drew Seminary, for the autumn quarter
of 1932.[145] While he was away, his associates at Chicago kept in
close touch with him by letter. Matthew Spinka wrote, "It must be
a great and glorious feeling to go back to one's seminary after one
has become great and famous."[146] Arthur C. McGiffert, Jr., sent Sweet
a pre-Christmas greeting in mid-November:

Why wait until Christmas to tell you how much we miss you around
here, and to remind you of the research that awaits your guiding hand?
Whether it is playing golf or standing around on my hind legs before
chapel, or walking along 58th Street, I am too frequently reminded of
your absence and wish you were back.[147]

Sweet had made the transition from DePauw to Chicago successfully.
By this time, Chicago was home.

But Drew also had plans for Sweet, as Sweet himself soon found
out. He wrote Case,

In a letter to Dean Mathews the other day I told him that I feared
President Brown was going to make me some kind of offer here at Drew.
Just what it is I do not know though I imagine from a former conversa-
tion with him and ex-President Tipple it was the Deanship of the Semi-
nary and the Church History job combined. To be frank and confidential
I am not greatly attracted to the place so far, for a number of reasons;
one is Lynn Harold Hough's professorship of Comprehensive Scholarship.
These professors of things in general are generally a thorn in the flesh.
I find myself very critical about a number of things about here, in comparison to the Divinity School.[148]

As the informal inquiries from Drew continued, Sweet wrote his
friend at DePauw, R. G. McCutchan, to ask his advice. McCutchan's
response merely underlined Sweet's rising prestige:

My feeling is that you should be in the place where you will be happiest. You do not need Chicago University or Drew or any other institution now. It is the institution that needs you. . . . You have already built a better mousetrap and the path will be beaten to your door, no matter where you are.[149]

Sweet continued as visiting professor at Drew during the autumn quarters of 1933 and 1934. The extended appointment was made possible by the fact that the University of Chicago administration was urging its faculty to take a quarter's vacation each year until the depression subsided.[150] The formal offer from Drew came during the autumn of 1934 from the new dean, Lynn Harold Hough, who offered Sweet the chair of church history and directorship of graduate studies at a salary of $7,000.[151]

At the news of the Drew offer, Sweet's Chicago associates deluged him with warm letters, practically begging him to return. Probably the most persuasive and influential of these communications came from Shirley Jackson Case, by then a close friend of Sweet and newly appointed dean of the Divinity School. He began by comparing the financial status of the two institutions, noting that the depression had forced Drew to instigate salary cuts, whereas there was no danger of such action at Chicago, at least in the immediate future. He further stated, "Chicago is primarily interested in giving you an opportunity to carry on research and to reduce your teaching load to the minimum." Case promised, "You can be sure that this will remain the chief emphasis here," referring to the difference between "the type of work in which you will continue to be engaged here . . . [and] the type to which you will have to give your time at Drew." Case also announced his intention to seek a salary increase for Sweet beginning the following academic year which would match the Drew offer of $7,000. Perhaps the most powerful of Case's inducements was the esteem in which he held Sweet. Recalling a conversation with the president of the university, he stated, "The President said, in almost these words, 'If Professor Sweet leaves, go out and get the best research scholar for the job.' When I told him you were that person, then he said to keep you."[152]

Sweet's final decision came when he asked Case if the Divinity

School would allow him to move the sources project to Drew. Case responded that the Divinity School had invested over $12,000 in the project and that it would remain at Chicago to be supervised by someone else should Sweet leave.[153] Two days later, Sweet wrote the dean at Drew Seminary declining his offer, giving as the reason the fact that he could not bring his research project to Drew, and noting "how much this project means to me."[154]

CONTINUED METHODIST INVOLVEMENT

The rising academic status of William Warren Sweet gave him increased prestige among his fellow Methodists as well. The editor of the Methodist publishing house, Abingdon Press, wrote him in 1937 after a misunderstanding, "Do not feel critical toward the Abingdon Press. The church cannot afford to have the premier historian of Methodism critical of the best church publishing house in existence."[155] This reputation encouraged Sweet to continue his active interest in church activities. Most of his efforts along these lines took place in the context of his work as a historian. His special concern was the reunion of the three branches of Methodism which had been separated since the slavery controversies which preceded the Civil War. His dissertation had dealt with the causes of the divisions. After he came to Chicago, he became a vigorous advocate of the use of Methodist history as a basis for reuniting the separated branches of Methodism. To this end, he wrote *Methodism in American History* in 1933, emphasizing that the historic bonds which united the three Methodisms were stronger than the issues which divided them.[156]

The work had been prepared at the invitation of a ministerial training committee of the Methodist church. It was to be used to acquaint ministers with the history of their own denomination. Upon its appearance it was adopted not only by the northern but also by the southern branch of the church as a required text for ministerial training. Sweet later attributed to this acceptance of a common past a significant part in bringing about the 1939 reunion of the three Methodisms:

The three Methodist churches which united in 1939 had come to the place where they were able to accept a common viewpoint on all the old controversial issues over which they had divided. . . . unification was made possible not because the old issues had been forgotten, but rather because they were now fully understood.[157]

Sweet himself, as the leading Methodist historian of the time, played no small part in bringing about what he called the "historical-mindedness" which helped lead to unification. In a later essay, Sweet attributed this new consciousness to "the entrance of the trained historian into the field of American church history," and pointed to the year 1912 as the time the first doctoral dissertations in the field began to appear.[158] He was of course describing the beginning of his own career.

Whether Sweet's historical works had the effect upon Methodist unification which he claimed would be difficult to assess. Sweet was a delegate to the Uniting Conference,[159] but the official minutes gave him no public recognition. At least it can be said that Sweet's treatment of Methodist history was a manifestation, if not a cause, of a growing spirit of optimism and unity within Methodism, and it is this facet of his Methodist works—as a reflection of the mood of a movement—which further enlarges his significance. Sweet's career coincides roughly with what may be called the triumphalist phase of American Methodist history, the era when the traditional Methodist condemnation of liquor became the law of the land, and when brick buildings and educated ministers became typical in Methodist churches. When reunion was achieved, it meant that Methodism was the largest and richest Protestant denomination, the unquestioned leader of the "mainstream" churches of America. Methodism may be said to have achieved the social prominence that its founder had feared when Bishop Edwin H. Hughes stated at the climactic closing of the Uniting Conference: "We find our lips uttering in affection the new name "The Methodist Church," glad that the scorn that once made it an epithet has been supplanted by the tribute that recognizes two centuries of a wide and holy service."[160]

It was this same triumphant spirit which led Sweet to emphasize successful churches in his treatment of American religion. It also provided him a point of contact with the optimistic and progressive mood which Mathews and Case transmitted to the Divinity School of the

University of Chicago. In that environment, Sweet's Methodist optimism expanded into an American Protestant optimism. He asserted,

Some day, I fully believe, in the not too distant future, our European
brethren will be awakened, and perhaps rudely so, to the fact that the
future of Protestant Christianity, just as the future of democracy, does
not lie with them but with the vigorous new churches across the western
ocean, born of the American frontier.[161]

The success of his own denomination inspired Sweet's confidence that
the future was indeed bright.

TEACHING ACTIVITIES

Aside from his publications, the area of Sweet's Chicago work
which most influenced the growing discipline of American religious
history was his training of the first large group of graduate students
in the field. Sweet was not known for the brilliance of his classroom
lectures at Chicago; but in order to place this fact in proper perspective, we must consider the kind of academic emphases prevalent
at the University of Chicago during those years. The educational
values of the university and of the Divinity School were illustrated
in Dean Case's reply to Sweet's request for a leave of absence during
the academic year 1935-36:

Our research enterprise for gathering sources for the history of
Christianity in America is one of the features of the Divinity School's
work that is most highly esteemed by the University administration, and
therefore I should hesitate to ask for a leave of absence for you during
1935-36, since that would mean suspending our research. The President
would, I suspect, be quite ready to have us reduce our teaching program
by allowing instructors to resign, but I am sure he would frown upon any
diminution of our research. This he regards as the chief task of a university. Some people might call him almost fanatical on the subject. Speaking
the other day in his characteristically explosive manner, he said, "I don't
care whether the Divinity School has a *teacher* of American Church History, or of any other subject." In other words, his primary interest is in
having us increase knowledge rather than simply peddle stock information. And so far as contact with students is concerned, the President
believes that the primary function of the teacher is to awaken the student's
interest in research and to equip him for that work. Merely to dole out

"embalmed" wisdom, as he terms it, is a task unworthy of a university. We could suspend your teaching for the year 1935-36, that being a lesser matter, but we cannot allow our research to lag for that period.[162]

Sweet's classroom manner at Chicago no doubt reflected something of this attitude. The lectures in his larger, survey courses were often informal affairs characterized by question-and-answer sessions in which Sweet found out very quickly who had mastered the details of the reading assignments. His lectures were liberally sprinkled with anecdotes "designed to illustrate the varying fate of the several denominations on the frontier."[163] Of course Sweet's informal approach to most of his survey classes did not mean that he could not give a very engaging lecture when he wanted to. For example, when he participated in a discussion of "The Religious Elements on the Frontier" at a meeting of historians in 1934, the minutes recorded that Sweet "held the audience to the last moment (an unusual thing for discussions)."[164] After he gave a speech at a local civic club in 1935, one of his audience wrote him, "Your address was one of the finest I have ever heard. You went to the very heart of the matter. It was simply thrilling."[165]

The courses which Sweet taught all dealt in some direct way with American religion, in contrast to those of his predecessor, Mode, who also had treated medieval and European topics. Thus Sweet's title as Professor of the History of American Christianity, the first such appointment in any university,[166] accurately described his teaching responsibilities.

In keeping with the university's emphasis on research, Sweet's major teaching activities took place in advanced graduate seminars composed of very small groups of students who were trained in historical method by dealing with primary source materials. The topics for these seminars were determined by whatever project Sweet was working on at the time. Often the curriculum would include a seminar dealing with the denominational materials Sweet was gathering in his sources project. The published descriptions of these courses noted that each student would be given a manuscript document which he would be expected to edit and criticize. The seminars thus made possible, at least in part, Sweet's prolific publications. He was always careful to acknowledge the help of his students, as the prefaces to all of his source books show.[167]

Sweet apparently attracted more Ph.D. students than the other members of the church history department. While he was a visiting professor at Drew during the autumn of 1932, Case wrote him, "We have a very promising group of students who are presenting themselves as candidates for higher degrees, and as usual most of them want to work in your field of specialization."[168] During his nineteen-year tenure at Chicago, he advised some thirty doctoral students who were specializing in American religious history, in addition to introducing to the field many others whose speciality was in another area. This large group of students later occupied positions in colleges and seminaries throughout the country and often taught the first courses in American church history offered at those institutions. Sweet's classes included such students as Winthrop Hudson, Sidney Mead, and Robert Handy, each of whom has become a noted historian of American religion. In addition to teaching students in the Divinity School, Sweet assisted in the direction of theses dealing with American religion in the history department of the university. Professors William E. Dodd and Marcus W. Jernegan of that department were particularly active in encouraging their students to study American religion and to do work with Sweet. The influence of Sweet's large number of students was recognized by his Abingdon editor in a letter to one of Sweet's critics:

Let me say that Dr. Sweet is recognized as the greatest authority on American Church History. He is the head of that Department in the Divinity School of the University of Chicago where he is training more students who are graduates of distinguished colleges than I suppose all other historians put together.[169]

This statement, in spite of its hyperbole, did contain some truth. Sweet did train the first group of graduate specialists in his field. In this sense he can legitimately be viewed as the founder of a professional academic discipline.

The dissertations which Sweet directed did not bear the stamp of a heavy-handed adviser. They were diverse in both topic and method.

Some stressed themes which were institutional, others were biographical, still others theological. Most of them gave careful attention to the economic and social factors which affected the religious topic they were tracing. All displayed thorough, sometimes painstaking, research. Some were written in a rather labored and pedantic style, but most were at least clear and straightforward. All of the dissertations dealt with Protestantism, and about half concentrated on a topic related to the frontier. The quality of these dissertations came to be recognized by American historians. One of them, Harvey Wish, in a review of one of Sweet's last works, referred to "the remarkably high-grade theses done by his numerous doctoral students."[170]

Sweet's accomplishments as a teacher were recognized by his contemporaries, among them Dean Willard L. Sperry of Harvard Divinity School. He invited Sweet to be a visiting professor and Dudleian Lecturer at Harvard during the spring of 1944, requesting that he "do something with the whole history of American Christianity—a field which has been shamefully neglected in this School."[171] Sweet's teaching must have had an impact, for in 1945 Sperry solicited recommendations from Sweet for a faculty appointment in American church history. Sweet provided him with a rather lengthy list of names, most of whom were his own students. Sperry responded, "I have looked over your list with great interest and can only congratulate you on the substantial contribution Chicago has made to the field."[172]

THE LATTER CHICAGO YEARS: A CHANGING WORLD

Sweet was not one to rest on his laurels, and his publishing pace continued throughout his Chicago tenure. In addition to continuous work on his source books, he began a project which he viewed as his *magnum opus*, a four-volume synthetic history of American religion. The first volume, *Religion in Colonial America*, appeared in 1942[173] and was a Religious Book Club selection. It received favorable criticism in scholarly journals and was pronounced by some the best treatment of the subject yet to appear.[174] Another significant work was *Revivalism in America*, a series of lectures given at Florida School of Religion in 1943.[175] The lectures were the idea of Shirley Jackson Case, who had retired from the deanship at Chicago in 1938 and had moved to Lakeland, Florida, to become the dean of the Florida School of Religion. The Sweets and the Cases had remained close friends after the Cases had left Chicago, and Case contrived the lectureship as a means of getting the Sweets to come for a long-awaited visit. *Revivalism in America* was one of Sweet's finest works. In it he described the different types of revivalism as parts of a theological spectrum, relating each to the social milieu in which it arose.

Changes at the Divinity School in the early 1940s made it seem like a different sort of place than it was when Sweet had arrived in 1927. Mathews and Case were gone and there were new faces on the faculty. Sweet described some of the differences in a letter to Case in 1944:

> There have been so many changes here at the University and especially in the Divinity School that I feel almost like a cat in a strange garret. Our Church History field now is made up of Dr. Mead, Hudson, Nichols and Neal, together with Deems and Lyttle beside myself. We had quite a flock of Ph.D. candidates coming up for their prelims during the summer and the examining committee was made up very largely of young men who had never sat in on doctor's examinations before. Like most young men who had received their own doctorates they were quite tough on the candidates and as a consequence seem to feel that the Ph.D. quota had been filled when they got their degree. They are all fine young men, however, and I am happy to be associated with them.[176]

Soon Sweet began to feel that the new faculty and administration were pursuing policies that would cause the school to decline. A new dean had arisen who emphasized ministerial education and Sweet was convinced, he wrote to Dean Sperry at Harvard, that "it will be a generation before Chicago will again attract men for graduate study in the same proportion as it has in the past."[177] He predicted that Chicago's falling mantle might soon be worn by Harvard.[178]

Part of the pessimism which these comments evidence may have been caused by the gloomy prospect of retirement, which was to occur in the spring of 1946. This impending event, so contrary to Sweet's personality and life-style, combined with the absence of old friends, clouded his last years at Chicago. Even his home was not the solace it once was, for as he wrote to a former student, "My wife and I are now alone, just where we started when we were married; for all the children are away."[179]

The fact that these years were overshadowed by World War II also had an effect on Sweet. He served on the Illinois War Finance Committee, devoting half of his time to his duties there and half to his teaching at the university. As a committee member he was responsible for stimulating sales of U.S. Bonds among immigrant nationalist groups in Illinois. This experience, plus the increasing specter of Nazi horrors, resulted in a two-part article in which Sweet explicitly repudiated the advocation in his early *History of Latin America* of racial, linguistic, and cultural unity as the basis for nationalism.[180] Instead, he now wrote on "Cultural Pluralism in the American Tradition," asserting that "there is need for the development of a sense of appreciation of all that the many nationals have contributed to the advancement of America."[181] Yet it was only half a conversion, for the article stopped far short of advocating true cultural pluralism. Sweet noted that "until recent years we meant by 'Americanization' elimination as far as possible of other cultural influences and values,"[182] but by the inclusion of the word "other" he revealed that he still maintained a normative concept of American values against which "foreign" ones were to be compared. What he did recommend was a kind of benign tolerance of "other" (i.e., non-British derived) cultures. For example, after describing the "dash, brilliance, cleverness, and emotion" of the Irish, he stated, "In spite of all their faults and failings, America would not be America without them."[183] He concluded the article by recommending "not the obliteration of all cultural differences, but rather the blending of all that is best from all cultures."[184] The key phrase here was "all that is best," for Sweet was willing to accede to "other" cultures not the right to retain all their values, but only the "best" ones, measured of course by an ideological standard to which Protestant hegemony was still the key.

SWEET'S CRUSADE

As Sweet's reputation grew during the Chicago years, he increasingly assumed the role of an evangelist proclaiming the value of American religious history. This was not a new position for him, for even at the beginning of his academic career, almost all of his published book reviews contained some statement about the need for historians to turn their attention to American religion. In 1924, for example, he had noted,

American religious history, as we have frequently been told in recent years, is one of the neglected fields. With a few notable exceptions, the American Church history which has been produced has been the work of the purely denominational writer, who too often has written from a strong partisan standpoint, while the so-called trained historian has to a greater or less degree ignored the subject.[185]

The following year he wrote, "The religious phase of American history deserves broad and sympathetic interpretation; instead it has never been adequately written and is very much misunderstood."[186] By the time he had accepted the Chicago appointment, he was emphasizing the benefits which such a study promised to historians: "The study of American religious history is not only important and profitable for its own sake, but also because of the sidelights and even direct illumination which such study will throw upon the social, political, and economic life of the nation."[187]

It is important to realize that Sweet never took the position that religious history was the sole or even the most important key to an understanding of American history in general. He avoided single cause hypotheses and was much more modest in his defense of his discipline. In an article which became his inaugural lecture at the University of Chicago, he stated very clearly the point he wanted to make on this issue:

This is not a plea that the American churches be given a place of first importance in the history of America, but rather a suggestion that the total life of the nation cannot adequately or truthfully be portrayed without giving them their due recognition. This neglect—perhaps contempt—for American church hisory on the part of the so-called "scientific" historian can be remedied only by the student of American church history, who must be equally scholarly and even more scientific; whose duty it shall be to point out clearly and conclusively the significance of American church history.[188]

Thus Sweet argued not for the priority of American religious history, but simply for its adoption by historians as a valid and profitable area of inquiry. The fact that his prize-winning *Tribune* essay on American history did not even mention religion is further evidence that he did not have an exalted view of its importance.

Sweet's remarks in his inaugural lecture can very accurately be seen as the academic charter of his Chicago career. His crusade for the recognition of his discipline continued, especially in the scores of book reviews which he published, where he never missed an opportunity to criticize the neglect or compliment the inclusion of religious factors in American history. Some historians listened, and Sweet began making converts. Ray A. Billington, for example, wrote to tell him what a help *The Story of Religions in America* had been in his own work, stating that he hoped to continue his studies "in the important field of church history which you have done so much to develop."[189]

It was largely an uphill battle which Sweet had to wage, for as Sidney Mead has pointed out, "When Professor Sweet began his work at the University of Chicago, American religious history as such was almost non-existent as a field of historical endeavor, and in graduate schools was generally frowned upon and discouraged."[190] Sweet acknowledged that the history department at Chicago was one of the few exceptions to this lamentable rule,[191] and his prodigious efforts in both publishing and teaching played a major role in making the Chicago situation less and less exceptional throughout the country. When Harvey Wish, in a review of one of Sweet's works, expressed appreciation for "the high scholarly standards which have made American religious history a major branch of historical scholarship,"[192] he was giving fitting tribute to what was in large part an achievement of Sweet's Chicago career.

5

Postretirement
1946-1959

ON THE EVENING of Tuesday, May 28, 1946, a testimonial dinner was held to honor William Warren Sweet on the occasion of his retirement from the University of Chicago. Sweet's colorful after-dinner speech that evening became his only published reflections about his life and career. The remarks were entitled "Every Dog Has His Day and I've Had Mine."[1] Sweet's address consisted primarily of reminiscences concerning his early years at Chicago. He described his surprising visit from Shirley Jackson Case when he was invited to come to Chicago, confessing that at that time he was ill prepared for the job, having had no courses in American church history; "for American church history as a field of teaching and research was at that time nonexistent." He also had serious reservations about coming to a "theological school" because he expected its academic standards to be lower than other professional and graduate schools. He soon discovered, however, that such reservations had no foundation "at least as far as Chicago was concerned."

In what was probably a barb directed at the increased interest in ministerial training at the Divinity School, Sweet flatly stated that his "chief interest in coming to the University was not to train preachers." Instead, he came "to develop an entirely new field of history" through research and the training of graduate students. In this effort he claimed some success, noting that "since that time American church history subjects have been increasingly chosen for Doctor's theses in every major American university." Sweet did not take all the credit for this accomplishment, for he generously noted the part the Divinity School and the university, including especially the history department, had played in developing his discipline. He claimed, "Nowhere in the United States was there another university in which such an experiment could have been inaugurated so successfully."

Sweet candidly confessed that at first he did not feel at home among the theologians at the Divinity School, a fact which he attributed to weaknesses in his own educational background. Noting that much of his problem was a lack of acquaintance with a new theological vocabulary, he stated, "I often wished that history might have developed an equally unintelligible jargon, for I am sure if it could have done so it would have been a much more respected discipline."

The most treasured memories of Sweet's Chicago tenure clearly belonged to that early period when Case and the spirited department which he had assembled were conquering the heights of academia. Sweet remembered that

the very atmosphere of the whole campus compelled us to keep busy, and the lights were burning in Swift Hall almost every night. Dr. Case set the pace, and we all did our best to be worthy of his leadership. One of the results was that between 1927 and 1944 there came from this body of church historians more than thirty volumes.

Sweet concluded his speech by looking to the future. He acknowledged that his "day" at the University was almost over: "in fact, it is rather late in the afternoon." But the afternoon, as he noted, was often the most pleasant part of the day:

Late afternoon is the playtime of the day. You can play tennis in the evening if you have a good heart and not too high blood pressure and if your children have not run off with all your tennis equipment. You can visit around among your children and from the sidelines watch them raising your grandchildren. There may be some teaching at other institutions to do and a great deal of reading you never had time for before and perhaps some writing that has long been planned.

Then, after a while, there will come the "twilight and evening bell."[2]

The leisurely pace which those closing statements prophesied, however, was never to occur while Sweet's health continued, as those who were close to him well knew. Literal retirement was altogether incompatible with his energetic personality, as Shirley Jackson Case noted in a letter to Sweet a year later:

Your industry astounds me! You are now an *emeritus*, which means that you are supposed to begin to take life easy, but apparently you have taken it as a stimulus to double your pace. You have earned a holiday. Already you have doubly justified my expectation that if I could persuade you to come to Chicago you would put American Church History on the map, which you certainly have done. That was an enterprise very dear to my heart and I shall always feel a deep sense of gratitude to you for the magnificent manner in which you have performed that task.[3]

Sweet took a faculty position at Garrett Seminary of Northwestern University after leaving the University of Chicago in the summer of 1946. The campus was in Evanston, a northern suburb of Chicago, and Sweet commuted there four days a week, still living in his Hyde Park apartment near the campus of the University on Chicago's South Side.[4] In addition to his Garrett teaching, he taught several courses at McCormick Seminary. After one year at Garrett, he was given a research fellowship at the Huntington Library in Southern California, where he and Mrs. Sweet spent the academic year 1947-48.

These were years when Sweet's prestige and influence were at their height. His Beckley Lectures which had been given in 1946 to an English audience were published in the United States in 1948, entitled *The American Churches*. They were brief interpretive essays sketching Sweet's view of the history of religious developments in America. The book which they compose remains the single work in which Sweet's characteristic theses were most clearly and concisely set forth. It was called by Kenneth S. Latourette "the best brief description of the Christianity of the United States." He added, "This book is the kind of excellent summary which can only be written by a master in the field."[5]

Sweet's works were increasingly being cited as definitive. When his friend Dean Willard Sperry of the Harvard Divinity School published his volume on American religion in 1946, he wrote Sweet, "Let me add once more that I appreciate the freedom of your pages which you so kindly gave me. I am afraid there are a half dozen pages of mine which are disguised plagiarism, since they are a condensation of longer pages in your books, but I am trusting you not to sue me. . . ."[6] Sweet's works became so authoritative in some circles that his conclusions about American religion were accepted at face value. Phrases such as "what Sweet establishes concerning the West"[7] became more common as sales figures for *The Story of Religions in America* hit their peak in the 1950s.[8]

After his term at the Huntington Library expired in the summer of 1948, Sweet accepted an appointment in the history department of Southern Methodist University in Dallas, Texas, the home of Sweet's son, William, Jr. The chairman of that department, Herbert Gambrell, had received his Ph.D. under Professor Dodd at Chicago, and had known Sweet there. Sweet's courses in the history department were very popular, for at SMU he enjoyed a high prestige indeed. During one semester, the lectures from his survey of American history were broadcast on radio "live" from the classroom.[9]

In Dallas he was flooded with invitations to speak before a wide variety of academic, professional, and civic groups. Gambrell asked him one day whether he noticed any differences between such audiences in Dallas and Chicago. Sweet responded, "Indeed I do. These Texans are better listeners, and they are irrevocably dedicated to *free speech.*" Gambrell missed the point and said something about the willingness of Texans to listen to divergent viewpoints. Sweet replied, "Yes, I suppose they will listen to anything if it doesn't cost them anything."

Gambrell's description of Sweet's personality during this period has a familiar ring:

Sweet was tall and of commanding appearance. He was genial but never palsy-walsy. Some students found him austere and peremptory. Colleagues who knew him well found him a delightful companion, a talented raconteur, and surprisingly well informed on a wide range of fields. His memory was usually accurate, and his characterizations of people he had known were brief and to the point. We marvelled at the number of "greats" among academicians and theologians and public men he had known personally, most favorably, a few unfavorably. His wit was ready and pointed, but never caustic. He enjoyed golf and fishing, was a delightful dinner guest, but mainly he was a badger for work.[10]

The last comment illustrates how little difference there really was between Sweet's earlier academic career and his so-called retirement. His continued vigor can be seen in a letter which he wrote to Dean Eugene B. Hawk of Perkins School of Theology at SMU in the summer of 1949. Sweet was then sixty-eight years old, yet he moved about his New Hampshire farm as though he were much younger:

I have been intending to report to you the past week and more, but after wielding a scythe for an hour or so each day for a week, getting our lawn in shape so that Dick could mow it with our new powermower, I'm in no frame of mind to write anyone. In fact my hands are just beginning to recover from a good batch of blisters. But now we have things pretty well under control and I have been able to get something done at my desk. The big manuscript I was reading for Dr. Anson Phelps Stokes has been completed and returned, and I understand it is now in the press. I have also begun the preparation of fourteen short articles for one of our Sunday School publications and there are other tasks awaiting me.[11]

The following year he added still more duties to his roster as he served as a visiting professor at the University of Texas, commuting the 150 miles to Austin by plane twice a week.

Although Professor Gambrell did not know it when he began to recruit Sweet to come to SMU, the president of the university, Umphrey Lee, had other plans for him. Perkins School of Theology at that time was headed by an aging dean whose study ended with a B.D. degree which he had received in 1909. The Perkins family was in the process of donating some eight million dollars to endow the school. Seminary enrollment was rising rapidly, and under the pressure of this growth, the dean had assembled a faculty which fell roughly into two factions—one composed mostly of younger faculty members who possessed earned doctorates from good universities and one primarily composed of those whom the dean had brought in from pastorates and who had remained, sometimes broadening their teaching commitments to include courses for which they were little qualified.[12]

There was naturally friction between these two groups, representing as they did two different philosophies of seminary education. With the retirement of the dean only three years away, it was an open question which of these two competing sets of values would govern the future development of the seminary. In an effort to tip the scales toward the first group and to mediate the various quarrels which were occurring, President Lee designated Sweet "Chairman of the Theology Faculty." Sweet was uncomfortable with this title, fearing it "such a nebulous term that it would be relatively easy for an assertive Dean to override . . ." He preferred the title, "Dean of the Faculty," but Lee would not change the designation.[13]

The position was created for Sweet and ceased to exist when he left it. His responsibilities, as defined in a memorandum of agreement between Dean Hawk and President Lee, included supervision of curriculum expansion, teaching assignments, and faculty appointments.[14] In this position Sweet made efforts, some successful, to restrict the teaching duties of faculty to areas in which they were expressly qualified.[15] Using his Chicago connections, he recruited several faculty members with outstanding academic credentials. He said, "Building a three and a half million dollar, seven building quadrangle is much easier than building a faculty equal to the buildings."[16] In an era of burgeoning enrollment, he made the frank comment, "We do not need more students; we need better students."[17] Screening procedures were soon introduced to determine the quality of candidates for admission. Another area of Sweet's concern was in making the seminary less academically isolated and more an integral part of the university. It disturbed him, for example, that the seminary operated on a completely different academic schedule than the rest of the university. He pointed out that this disparity meant that "non-theological students cannot take our courses nor do our students take courses in other departments."[18] He was particularly sensitive to this issue because his history department courses dealing with American religion could be attended by seminary students only with great inconvenience.

As the appointment of the new dean approached, Sweet showed

a predictable concern. He noted, "President Lee is determined the new Dean must be a scholar as well as a preacher, though there is considerable pressure being brought to bear to take a man from the pastorate . . ."[19] Sweet successfully encouraged Lee to appoint as dean Merrimon Cuninggim, whose tenure, beginning in 1951, was a boon to the academic stature of the school.

Sweet retired from his SMU positions in the spring of 1952. This second retirement was again the occasion for a testimonial dinner, but this one was somewhat more exuberant than the one in Chicago, Sweet's accomplishments being more unusual at SMU. The president of the university, Umphrey Lee, was the toastmaster, and Professor Gambrell, who had initiated the efforts to bring Sweet to the campus, gave the eulogy. Dean Cuninggim also spoke, but the political exigencies of the occasion made it impossible for him to tell the whole story of Sweet's contributions at SMU. The seminary's debt to Sweet had to be acknowledged in private. Cuninggim thus wrote Sweet at his New Hampshire farm the following summer to express his gratitude. He apologized for not saying at the dinner "all that could have been said," stating,

I did not feel that I could describe the skill with which you worked with various people who didn't altogether understand or appreciate the standards you held or the goals you sought for the School. . . . So the full truth couldn't be stated—but the full truth as I know it is that you, more than anyone else during the years of your residence here, preserved and enlarged the chance which this School has for real stature some day. Your work here will be appreciated more, rather than less, as the years go by. If it would have been somewhat impolite to say all this on the occasion of the banquet, at least I want to let you know personally.[20]

Herbert Gambrell noted that Sweet had the same kind of effect throughout the university: "His brief stay at SMU was a greater stimulus than he probably realized to the faculty of a college trying to become a university. . . . The example he set and assiduity with which he did whatever he undertook was a real incentive to many of the budding scholars."[21]

In the year of his second retirement, the manuscript which he had begun at the Huntington Library in 1948 was published. *Religion in the Development of American Culture 1765-1840* was Sweet's finest book-length historical work, covering as it did the period from which his distinctive theses were all derived. It was written as the second volume in his proposed four-volume *magnum opus* covering the entire history of American religion. It began by quoting J. Franklin Jameson's 1907 presidential address before the American Historical Association: "Of all the means of estimating American character . . . the pursuit of religious history is most complete."[22] Sweet's volume was a direct answer to Jameson's recommendations.

The first two chapters surveyed American religion in the Revolutionary generation. Chapter three, "Breaking Old World Ties," treated the forming of independent American denominations after the Revolution. Chapter four, "Religion Follows the Frontier," presented Sweet's connection between church polity and frontier growth. Chapter five, "Barbarism vs. Revivalism," emphasized the moral structure which revivals brought to the undisciplined frontier. Chapter six, "Religion and Our Cultural Foundations," stressed the educational institutions founded by religious groups. Chapter seven, "The Revolt against Calvinism," illustrated the Arminian trends in the development of theology on the frontier. Chapters eight and nine described frontier benevolent institutions and utopian movements.

The broad outlines of Sweet's story were identical to those contained in his previous synthetic works, yet this volume displayed a unity and a sophistication which marked it as the work of a mature scholarly craftsman. It remains in print to this day, and is still useful as a history of Protestant expansion in the Mississippi Valley. It was the last of his proposed four-volume series to be completed. Only a chapter of the third volume, which was to have dealt with the Civil War period, had been completed at the time of his death in 1959.

Academic critics of Sweet began to emerge in the 1950s, as one should expect in any growing discipline. Whitney R. Cross published his important work, *The Burned-over District: The Social and Intellectual History of Enthusiastic Religion in Western New York*, in 1950, successfully arguing that neither revivalism nor utopianism was a frontier phenomenon as Sweet had implied, and questioning some of Sweet's connections between denominational polity and frontier success.[23] Sweet's successor at Chicago, Sidney E. Mead, put significant distance between himself and his teacher in a 1953 article which questioned both Sweet's focus and his method.[24] H. Shelton Smith, in an otherwise appreciative review, stated, "Dr. Sweet's Turnerian thesis is mostly a house built on sand."[25] Many of these critics failed to perceive the important differences between Sweet and Turner.[26] Virtually all seasoned academicians continued, however, to respect Sweet's accomplishments. Winthrop S. Hudson, for example, stated in 1953, "Professor Sweet in a very real sense is the father of American church history and no one has contributed more to the growing recognition of the importance of church life and activity in the social and cultural history of America."[27]

After his retirement from SMU at the age of seventy-one, Sweet took a faculty position in the history department of Pomona College in Claremont, California, for the academic year 1952-53. Here he had access to the Huntington Library, where he worked on his history of Virginia Methodism.[28] Following the year in Claremont, he returned to Dallas to continue his writing. He had sold his Chicago apartment and New Hampshire farm, and Dallas was now considered home. During this period he took an interest in the SMU Press, donating some of his royalties to it and eventually giving it a fund of some $5,000.[29]

In the autumn of 1955, the Sweets journeyed to Mills College in Oakland, California, where he served as a professor of history for a year. By the time they returned to Dallas the following summer, it was apparent that Sweet's health had begun to deteriorate. He occasionally had difficulty maintaining his balance, and sometimes fell while walking. The first symptoms of Parkinson's Disease had appeared. There was a slight prospect of improvement with surgery, but the operation was very dangerous and could prove fatal. Sweet wanted to have the surgery immediately, but Louise and his son William persuaded him to fly to Boston to consult with his nephew, William H. Sweet, a well-known neurosurgeon at Massachusetts General Hospital. After several weeks of intensive examinations, it was Dr. Sweet's opinion that his uncle's age and general condition rendered surgery too risky.

Professor and Mrs. Sweet returned to Dallas, where she continued to care for him. Even though his health continued to decline, "he continued to be ambulatory and steadfastly refused a wheelchair or

cane, although he fell constantly and often bruised himself badly."[30]
His physical deterioration, complicated by arteriosclerosis, was perhaps
harder on his family than on Sweet himself. It was difficult for them
to see him physically humbled when they remembered the vitality
which had been so characteristic of his life and career. Sweet, however,
characteristically resisted pessimism, as can be seen in one of his last
surviving letters:

I am sorry to report that my unsteadiness seems to have increased
which interferes with my walking, and when I fall, it disturbs all the
family though I think I have become an expert in that performance.
When I fall, I have learned to break the impact, and so far I have had
no injury from it. . . .[31]

His son William summarized his attitude: "He felt, I think, that he
had lived a full life and that he had received from it everything that
he had a right to expect and that he should not resent the fact that
it might be over."[32] It was the same attitude that he had expressed in
his retirement speech at Chicago. He had had his day.

He spent the Christmas holidays of 1958 at the home of his son
in Dallas, and it was there that death came quickly and quietly on
January 3, 1959. After a splendid, eulogistic funeral in the beautiful
chapel of Perkins School of Theology, he was buried on a cool, clear
afternoon beneath the shade of some large trees at Restland Memorial
Park on the northern outskirts of Dallas.

The life of William Warren Sweet revolved about an unusually
consistent set of ideals from beginning to end. Each of the social
settings in which he lived and worked was amenable to those ideals,
for Sweet was no iconoclast. The notable accomplishments which the
previous chapters have chronicled thus do not exhaust the significance
of Sweet's career, because his representativeness makes his life a win-
dow through which we may view important segments of American
history.

Within the historical profession, Sweet represents the awakening
of American historians to the study of the religious bases of American
culture. Among historians of American religion, Sweet illustrates the

peak of the Baird-Dorchester-Bacon tradition of identifying American religion with a Protestant mainstream, as well as the partial emancipation of the discipline from ecclesiastical triumphalism. In the academic world, Sweet manifests the rise of an assertive midwestern consciousness so typical of the early University of Chicago, which proclaimed to the bastions of eastern culture that the real America lay beyond their horizons. Within Methodism, Sweet represents the optimism of the reunion years when it seemed that the future of institutional Methodism, largest of the Protestant denominations, would be even brighter than its glorious past. In the larger context of American social history, Sweet exemplifies the ideals of a religious, moral, and social order which were generally characteristic of pre-urban, Anglo-Saxon, Protestant society in America.

The history of this social order has been told by, among others, Robert Handy and Martin Marty (to name two historians with Sweet pedigrees), and needs no repetition here. The important point which Sweet illustrates is that such a social order was conceived as unitary, not pluralistic, in its ideology. In Sweet's vocabulary, "typically American" institutions were in fundamental agreement on moral, religious, and social values.

As we have seen, the social order of frontier Kansas gave to Sweet's construction of American religious history its distinctive midwestern, frontier, Protestant, and Methodist cast. Both the strengths and the weaknesses of Sweet's synthesis stem from this origin. Because his synthesis was informed by the realities of his own experience, it contains insights about American history which are true and valid, as far as they go. There is no question that at one time Protestant hegemony was not an assumption but a historical fact in most areas of the United States. And there are certain characteristics of Methodism which continue to lead such distinguished historians as Jaroslav Pelikan to refer to it as "the most American of churches."[33] Thus Sweet's generalizations about the effects upon American life of a Methodist-led, Protestant mainstream are in many instances largely correct. But to look at the other side of the ledger, because Sweet's synthesis was primarily informed only by the realities of his own experience, it was simply too selective and limited to be called *the* story of religion in America. Sweet constructed his works to answer the question, "How did we get here?" But by "we" he meant a particular group of Protestant denominations. Roman Catholics, Lutherans, Jews, blacks, and others who were not a part of the question were naturally not a part of the answer.

The "we" of today's historians is of course considerably broader, because American society is now more explicitly pluralistic. Sweet and most of his contemporaries could not see from our vantage point. They perpetuated concepts of American society which more properly belonged in a previous era before massive non-British immigration radically changed the social composition of the United States. By the mid-twentieth century, and certainly by the election of 1960, it was clear to most observers of American society that any adequate historical treatment of their subject would have to have a considerably broader focus than the so-called Protestant mainstream. Sweet was not among those observers, nor should we expect him to be, for his concepts of American society were formed in quite a different milieu.

The extraordinary success of Sweet's academic career exhibits the extent to which Protestant hegemony continued to be an assumed social fact in those contexts where his career was spent. Even into the twentieth century, when the handwriting was already on the Ellis Island wall, a large segment of upper-crust American society continued to identify American culture as necessarily Protestant. The extraordinary tenacity of such a connection was present far beyond Baldwin, Kansas. It permeated the University of Chicago during Sweet's years there. It permeated Methodism and other Anglo-Saxon, Protestant churches. It permeated the historical profession and American universities at least until the mid-twentieth century. Sweet was able to construct a historical synthesis of American religion which was widely acclaimed in spite of its nonrepresentativeness precisely because it rested on concepts which were congruent with his and his colleagues' social backgrounds.

Appendix A

While this familiar cliché which I have taken as my text may seem to you to have been chosen in a flippant mood, yet it was not so intended. I have chosen it because it expresses my attitude toward my retirement better than any other phrase with which I am familiar.

In the first place, I do not feel resentful at the necessity of retiring at sixty-five. Rather, I think in many respects it is a wise provision. Although some men may be at the very peak of their powers at sixty-five—and, of course, I am—yet we are all perfectly aware of the fact that they cannot remain so long thereafter. Doddering old men are seldom able to see themselves as others see them. That was one of the reasons why my wife and I decided to move away, *Deus volens,* from the University community on our retirement, not because our affection for the University or for our University friends

---

* William Warren Sweet, "Every Dog Has His Day and I've Had Mine," *University of Chicago Divinity School News* 13 (August 1, 1946): 4-8.

had grown less but because we would prefer to be remembered as we were than as we are sure to become. What is true of us will be true of you all. Time will attend to that.

The realization that I have reached the age when I can claim the right to reminisce has come to me with something of a shock. In my day I have been compelled to listen to the reminiscing of other aging men, and too often it has been a heavy cross to bear. But, nevertheless, I now claim the right to do just that, at least for a few moments, which, I hope, you will bear with becoming Christian fortitude.

I
MY DAY

My day at the University of Chicago has been nineteen years long. As I look back, a certain day in the spring of 1926 is vivid in my memory. In the late afternoon of a beautiful Indiana spring day a Cadillac drew up before our house and a tall gentleman alighted. I mentioned the Cadillac because none of my friends were driving cars of that make at that time. At once I surmised that something unusual was in the wind. And there was. This tall, lithe gentleman proved to be Shirley Jackson Case, and within fifteen minutes he had offered me a professorship in American church history at the University of Chicago. There had been no correspondence about the matter, and I was not aware that the University of Chicago had ever heard of me. When I suggested that it seemed rather sudden and that he probably did not know much about me, Dr. Case remarked, "We know all there is to know about you." While I did not accept at once, I did accept the next year and began my work at the University in the autumn of 1927.

Now I have some confessions to make, which perhaps should have been made long ago.

The first is that I was not prepared for the job. Nor, as far as I know, was there anyone else prepared for it if by preparation is meant having had courses in the fields; for American church history as a field of teaching and research was at that time nonexistent. I had never taken a course in American church history, and as far as I know there were few if any such courses offered anywhere. My graduate study at Columbia University and at the University of Pennsylvania had been in the field of Semitics, in which I received the Master's degree (1909), and in European and American history, in which I received the doctorate (1912). I had never thought of teaching church history until that spring afternoon when Dr. Case broached the matter to me in our Greencastle living-room.

The teaching experience I had had before coming to the University had all been in general European and American history, and, with the exception of some graduate students I had had at Syracuse and Northwestern universities, and at the University of Washington, where I had been a visiting professor during several summers, my teaching had been of an undergraduate nature. It was therefore with considerable trepidation that I began my work here on the graduate level and mainly with theological students. I confess, too, that theological schools had no great attraction for me, for I had the idea—an idea which was then much in vogue and still is in some quarters—that theological schools were generally on a distinctly lower scholastic level than other professional and graduate schools. This I soon discovered was a fallacy at least as far as Chicago was concerned.

A second confession I am impelled to make is that my chief interest in coming to the University was not to train preachers. Rather I came because there was offered me here a chance of helping to develop an entirely new field of history. In fact, that was the thing which Dr. Case had stressed. I was to be given an adequate research fund; part of my work was to build up American church history in the library, and I was challenged to make it the best in the country. I was to collect and publish sources, and I was promised that in carrying on this work I was to have secretarial help and, when possible, research assistants. And the best thing about it was that it all came true. Throughout my nineteen years here at the University I have never made a valid request for the advancement of my work that has not been granted, and seemingly with great willingness.

Nowhere in the United States was there another university in which such an experiment could have been inaugurated so successfully. Before my coming to the University, Professors William E. Dodd and Marcus M. Jernegan had for several years been encouraging students to do research in this field, and several notable Doctor's dissertations had already been produced. In fact, I think that Professor

Dodd's presence at the University had more to do with my coming than any other single factor. Everywhere else, with one or two notable exceptions, Doctor's theses in the field of American church history were discouraged by the history departments on the ground that such subjects could not be treated with sufficient objectivity. Here I did not have that absurd position to face in the history department. And since that time American church history subjects have been increasingly chosen for Doctor's theses in every major American university. Chicago no longer has a monopoly on research in that field.

One of the principal services that has been rendered here at the University through the emphasis that has been placed upon teaching and research in American church history has been to make available to the general American historian such materials as will enable him to appreciate adequately the part played by religion in the development of American civilization. It has been most interesting to me to note that many recent American history textbooks bear such titles as the *History of American Civilization* or the *History of American Culture*, indicating that the scope of American history has been broadened to include the great civilizing and cultural forces which formerly were almost completely omitted. And I believe that what we have been doing in American church history here had something to do with this new emphasis.

I have still another confession which at long last I have been given the courage to make. For at least the first ten years of the nineteen that I have been a member of this faculty, I had the feeling that I really did not belong. The reason for this feeling, as I look back at it, was something like this. It was just twenty-one years after my graduation from Drew Theological Seminary that I joined the Divinity School faculty, and during those twenty-one years theological education in the United States had undergone a complete transformation. I had never been exposed to religious education or to the psychology of religion or to the philosophy of religion or to the sociology of religion. When I was a student in the seminary, the study of theology was at low ebb; but, when I joined the faculty here, theology was undergoing a new birth. All these new disciplines had their own jargon, and the air about here was blue with it, or whatever color air becomes under such conditions. And, by the way, the definition of "jargon" found in Webster is "to emit confused or unintelligible sounds; to talk unintelligibly, or in a harsh and noisy manner." It took me a good ten years to get an inkling of what it was all about, but during the last nine years I have begun to feel a little more at home. During that long period of my apprenticeship in these new disciplines, I often wished that history might have developed an equally unintelligible jargon, for I am sure if it could have done so it would have been a much more respected discipline. Another handicap under which history had labored is that it has never professed to furnish a quick remedy for the ills of the world. It knows too much about man's long record. But it has, I think, served as a balance wheel to keep the theological engine from burning out all its cylinders.

When I came to the University nineteen years ago, I came to join Shirley Jackson Case, W. E. Garrison, and John T. McNeill in the University of Chicago, Matthew Spinka and Wilhelm Pauck of the Chicago Theological Seminary, and Charles Lyttle of Meadville Theological School, who constituted the largest group of church historians to be found in any university center. And it was a busy and cooperative group. The very atmosphere of the whole campus compelled us to keep busy, and the lights were burning in Swift Hall almost every night. Dr. Case set the pace, and we all did our best to be worthy of his leadership. One of the results was that between 1927 and 1944 there came from this body of church historians more than thirty volumes.

II

AFTERNOON

And now my day at the University is about over; in fact, it is rather late in the afternoon. But the afternoon can be and ought to be the most pleasant part of the day, and we, my wife and I, intend to make it so. There are so many things that can be done in the afternoon that one does not think of even trying to do in the morning. Late afternoon is the playtime of the day. You can play tennis in the evening if you have a good heart and not too high blood pressure and if your children have not run off with all your tennis equipment. You can visit around among your children and from the sidelines watch them raising your grandchildren. There may be some teaching at other institutions to do and a great deal of reading you never had time for before and perhaps some writing that has long been planned.

Then, after a while, there will come the "twilight and evening bell."

Appendix B

SWEET'S LETTER TO PRESIDENT TRUMAN*

October 20, 1950

The Honorable Harry S Truman
President of the United States
Washington, D. C.

My dear President Truman:

I am addressing you on the matter of your announced intention of appointing a regular and permanent United States diplomatic representative to the Vatican. I write not as a bitter partisan, but as a student of American History, particularly in its cultural and religious phase. For twenty years I was a member of the faculty of the University of Chicago, where I helped to develop the new field of American Church History. In that connection, for the past several years I have given a course on Church and State, usually at the graduate level, and I believe I have some competence to speak to you on the matter of

---

* William Warren Sweet to President Harry S Truman, October 20, 1950, Sweet Papers SMU, 3:24.

your proposal. (See my *Religion in Colonial America*, Chapter X, Scribners, 1942; and also my Dudleian Lectures at Harvard University on *Natural Religion and Religious Liberty.*)

In the first place, such an appointment as you propose would undoubtedly constitute a serious breach in the wall of separation between Church and State. As Anson Phelps Stokes has clearly shown in his recent volumes, *Church and State in the United States* (3 vols., Harpers, 1950), if the wall of separation is not maintained all our great freedoms are in danger. As has been well stated recently, all of our freedoms constitute one bundle, and if one is destroyed the whole bundle is destroyed. To give special consideration to one Church, as a national policy, would undoubtedly produce a chain of events of serious import.

In the second place, such an appointment would introduce into American politics the bane of European politics, clericalism and anti-clericalism, and once introduced it would tend to become a permanent cause of mounting bitterness. I would regret to have your name connected in the history of our time with such a thing as that. Although an independent voter as a usual thing, I not only voted for you, but have supported most of your policies, particularly your foreign and labor policy.

Thirdly, I would like to call to your attention the fact that such an appointment, while undoubtedly pleasing to the great city political machines, might well be a cause of division in your own party in the Southern states. I need not remind you that the first and most important of the five great Baptist principles is the complete separation of Church and State, and I might also add that all of the great churches in America likewise subscribe to that principle, save one.

With all good wishes, I am

Most sincerely yours,

William W. Sweet
Chairman of the Faculty

WWS/mfw

Notes

INTRODUCTION

1. Timothy L. Smith, *Revivalism and Social Reform* (New York: Abingdon Press, 1957), p. 9.

2. "Father of American Church History Dies," *Christian Century* 76 (January 21, 1959): 71.

3. Edwin S. Gaustad, "Religion in America: History and Historiography," American Historical Association Pamphlet 260 (Washington, D.C.: American Historical Association, 1973), pp. 52-53.

4. William A. Clebsch, "A New Historiography of American Religion," *Historical Magazine of the Protestant Episcopal Church* 32(1963): 225-57.

5. Jerald C. Brauer, "Changing Perspectives on Religion in America," in *Reinterpretation in American Church History*, ed. Jerald C. Brauer (Chicago: University of Chicago Press, 1968), pp. 1-28.

6. Henry F. May, "The Recovery of American Religious History," *American Historical Review* 70 (1964-65): 79-92.

7. Sydney E. Ahlstrom, *A Religious History of the American People* (New Haven: Yale University Press, 1972), p. 10.

8. William Warren Sweet, *American Culture and Religion* (Dallas: Southern Methodist University Press, 1951), p. 74; William Warren Sweet, *The Story of Religions in America*, 1st ed. (New York: Harper & Bros., 1930), pp. 1-2.

9. Sweet, *American Culture*, p. 76.

10. An influential moment in this trend appears to have been the publication of J. H. Randall, Jr., and G. Haines IV, "Controlling Assumptions in the Practice of American Historians," in *Theory and Practice in Historical Study: A Report of the Committee on Historiography*, Social Science Research Council, Bulletin no. 54 (New York, 1946).

11. Brauer, "Changing Perspectives," p. 7; Ahlstrom, *A Religious History*, p. 10.

12. The best is still Sidney E. Mead's "Professor Sweet's Religion and Culture in America," *Church History* 22 (March 1953): 33-49, in which Mead interprets his professor in terms of the combination of two disparate intellectual influences—Frederick Jackson Turner's thesis-centered method focusing on the American frontier and John Bach McMaster's enumerative method focusing on factual data. Henry W. Bowden, "Modern Developments in the Interpretation of Church History," *Historical Magazine of the Protestant Episcopal Church* 43 (1974): 105-23, gives an accurate summary of Sweet's views, suggesting that Sweet's veneration of frontier Methodism might have arisen from a sense of bewilderment in "a time of national insecurity," as an effort to recover the stability of a past era. Archie H. Jones, "American Protestantism and the Science of History" (Ph.D. diss., University of Chicago, 1954), devotes some twenty pages to Sweet, relating his career to the "Chicago school" of religious historians gathered by Shailer Mathews and Shirley Jackson Case. Jonathan A. Lindsey, "A Critical Evaluation of William Warren Sweet as a Writer of American Church History" (Th.D. diss., Southern Baptist Theological Seminary, 1967), occasionally offers legitimate summaries of Sweet's conclusions. William F. Riley, Jr., "The Influence of Turner's Frontier Thesis upon American Religious Historiography" (M.A. thesis, Western Kentucky University, 1974), alleges Sweet's congruence with Turner.

CHAPTER ONE

1. William H. Sweet, *A History of Methodism in Northwest Kansas* (Salina, Kansas: Kansas Wesleyan University, 1920), pp. 6-7.

2. This fact, together with much of the subsequent biographical detail, is taken from Sweet, *History of Methodism*, pp. 1-12.

3. William F. Zornow, *Kansas: A History of the Jayhawk State* (Norman, Oklahoma: University of Oklahoma Press, 1957), pp. 137-38.

4. Ibid., pp. 164-65.

5. Upon his arrival President Sweet, finding that the music department had no piano, donated a horse and $100 to buy one. While a professor, he had given land to the school to retire a debt. In 1881 he donated $100 for a similar purpose. (Sweet, *History of Methodism*, pp. 13, 14, 16, 20.)

6. Homer K. Ebright, *The History of Baker University* (Baldwin, Kansas: Baker University, 1951), p. 116; Sweet, *History of Methodism*, p. 23.

7. Zornow, *Kansas*, p. 165.

8. Ibid.

9. Ebright, *History of Baker University*, pp. 30, 40.

10. Zornow, *Kansas*, pp. 139-40; Robert W. Baughman, *Kansas in Maps* (Topeka, Kansas: Kansas State Historical Society, 1961), p. 78.

11. Horace Greeley, *An Overland Journey from New York to San Francisco* (New York: C. M. Saxton, Barker & Co., 1860), p. 39.

12. *Baldwin Criterion*, March 20, 1884.

13. Supplement to the *Baldwin Criterion*, April 1885.

14. Zornow, *Kansas*, pp. 174-75.

15. Don W. Holter, *Fire on the Prairie: Methodism in the History of Kansas* (n.p.: Editorial Board of the Kansas Methodist History, 1969), pp. 101, 145.

16. Ibid., pp. 110-11.

17. Ibid., p. 120.

18. M. G. Hamm, *Central Christian Advocate*, January 18, 1893, quoted in Holter, *Fire on the Prairie*, p. 121.

19. Holter, *Fire on the Prairie*, p. 124.

20. Ibid., pp. 87-96, 154-66.

21. *Topeka Capitol*, June 26, 1932.

22. *Kansas State Census of 1885*, 79:95.

23. Ibid., p. 136.

24. Ibid., vol. 81, schedule 8.

25. *Baldwin Ledger*, December 12, 1885.

26. *Baker University Catalogue* (1862), quoted in Ebright, *History of Baker University*, p. 69.

27. Will Hair to Paul W. Sweet, n.d., quoted in Sweet, *History of Methodism*, p. 4.

28. William A. Irwin, "William Warren Sweet," typewritten (eulogy delivered at Sweet's funeral in Dallas, 1959), p. 1. This work was compiled from an interview with Sweet's widow, Louise Neill Sweet, shortly after her husband's death in 1959.

29. Florence L. Snow, description of William H. Sweet, quoted in Ebright, *History of Baker University*, pp. 103-4.

30. Sweet, *History of Methodism*, p. 47.

31. Ruby P. Bramwell, *City on the Move: The Story of Salina* (Salina, Kansas: Survey Press, 1969), pp. 152-58.

32. Jack W. VanDerhoff, *The Time Now Past: Kansas Wesleyan University, 1886-1961* (Salina, Kansas: Kansas Wesleyan University, 1962), pp. 16-17.

33. U.S. Department of the Interior, Census Office, *Compendium of the Eleventh Census: 1890*, vol. 1, *Population* (Washington, D.C.: Government Printing Office, 1892), p. 171.

34. William H. Milburn, *Lance, Cross, and Canoe* (New York: Derby & Jackson, 1857).

35. William Warren Sweet, *The Rise of Methodism in the West* (New York: Methodist Book Concern, 1920), p. 33.

36. Paul R. Sweet to James L. Ash, Jr., January 28, 1975.

37. William W. Sweet, Jr., to James L. Ash, Jr., January 23, 1975.

38. Russel B. Nye, *Midwestern Progressive Politics* (New York: Harper & Row, Harper Torchbooks, 1965), p. 63.

39. Holter, *Fire on the Prairie*, pp. 141-43.

40. William A. White, "What's the Matter with Kansas?" *Emporia Weekly Gazette*, August 20, 1896, p. 1.

41. *Salina Daily Republican-Journal*, January 19, 1899.

42. Paul W. Sweet, "Biographical Introduction," in Sweet, *History of Methodism*, p. 31.

43. Peter L. Berger and Thomas Luckmann, *The Social Construction of Reality* (New York: Doubleday, 1966), p. 131.

44. Ibid., pp. 136-38.

45. Thorstein Veblen, "The Country Town," in *The Portable Veblen*, ed. Max Lerner (New York: Viking Press, 1961), p. 407, quoted in Page Smith, *As a City Set upon a Hill: The Town in American History* (New York: Alfred A. Knopf, 1966), pp. vii-viii.

46. Smith, *As a City Set upon a Hill*, p. 53.

47. William A. Quale, "Eulogy of Werter R. Davis," quoted in Ebright, *History of Baker University*, p. 62.

48. Jean B. Quandt, *From the Small Town to the Great Community: The*

Social Thought of Progressive Intellectuals (New Brunswick, N.J.: Rutgers University Press, 1970).

49. William Warren Sweet, "The Churches as Moral Courts of the Frontier," *Church History* 2 (January 1933): 2-21.

CHAPTER TWO

1. Elizabeth Sweet Hix to James L. Ash, Jr., January 21, 1975.
2. Don W. Holter, *Fire on the Prairie: Methodism in the History of Kansas* (n.p.: Editorial Board of the Kansas Methodist History, 1969), p. 162.
3. Laurence R. Veysey, *The Emergence of the American University* (Chicago: University of Chicago Press, 1965), pp. 36-37.
4. *Annual Catalogue of the Kansas Wesleyan University for the Twelfth Academic Year, 1897-98* (Salina, Kansas: Kansas Wesleyan University, 1898), pp. 27-31.
5. *Wesleyan Advance* 10 (January 1899): 10.
6. Manly J. Mumford, "The Educational System of the Methodist Episcopal Church," *Wesleyan Advance* 9 (April 1898): 107.
7. *Songs of Kansas Wesleyan University* (Salina, Kansas: Kansas Wesleyan University, 1909), p. 20.
8. *Salina Weekly Republican-Journal,* October 1, 1897.
9. Hamlin Garland, *Crumbling Idols* (Chicago: Stone & Kimball, 1894).
10. C. N. Poe, "The Kansan in Literature," *Wesleyan Advance* 10 (February 1899): 6.
11. Rudyard Kipling, "The White Man's Burden," quoted in "The Changing Policy of the United States," *Wesleyan Advance* 10 (March 1899): 5-6.
12. Stephen C. Fink, Director of Alumni Services, Kansas Wesleyan University, to James L. Ash, Jr., October 7, 1974.
13. *Annual Catalogue of the Kansas Wesleyan University,* p. 50.
14. Ibid., pp. 27-28.
15. *Fifty-sixth Catalogue of Ohio Wesleyan University* (Delaware, Ohio: Ohio Wesleyan University, 1900), p. 113; *Fifty-seventh Catalogue of Ohio Wesleyan University* (Delaware, Ohio: Ohio Wesleyan University, 1901), p. 99.
16. A. W. Chase, *Dr. Chase's Third, Last and Complete Receipt Book and Household Physician* (Detroit: F. B. Dickerson, 1902).
17. Interview with Paul R. Sweet, June 24, 1974.
18. Ibid.
19. The Junior Class of Ohio Wesleyan University, *The Bijou* (Columbus, Ohio: Champlin Press, 1901), p. 370.
20. *The College Transcript,* September 28, 1901.
21. Interview with Paul R. Sweet.
22. *The College Transcript,* November 27, 1901.
23. Ibid.
24. Interview with Paul R. Sweet.
25. Richard Hofstadter and Walter Metzger, *The Development of Academic Freedom in the United States* (New York: Columbia University Press, 1955), pp. 316-19.
26. Henry C. Hubbart, *Ohio Wesleyan's First Hundred Years* (Delaware, Ohio: Ohio Wesleyan University, 1943), p. 87.
27. Junior Class of Ohio Wesleyan, *Bijou,* pp. 10-11.
28. Hubbart, *Ohio Wesleyan's First Hundred Years,* p. 104.
29. William A. Irwin, "William Warren Sweet" (Eulogy delivered at Sweet's funeral in Dallas, 1959), p. 1.

30. Hubbart, *Ohio Wesleyan's First Hundred Years*, p. 99.

31. My estimate based on the data in Hubbart, *Ohio Wesleyan's First Hundred Years*, p. 93.

32. Ibid., p. 91.

33. Ibid., p. 95.

34. Ibid., p. 107.

35. Ibid.

36. Paul W. Sweet, "Biographical Introduction," in William H. Sweet, *A History of Methodism in Northwest Kansas* (Salina, Kansas: Kansas Wesleyan University, 1920), p. 4.

37. *Year Book of Drew Theological Seminary, 1904-1905* (Madison, N.J.: Drew Theological Seminary, 1905), pp. 12, 30-41.

38. Ibid., p. 14; *Year Book of Drew Theological Seminary, 1905-1906* (Madison, N.J.: Drew Theological Seminary, 1906), p. 13.

39. Official Transcript of William Warren Sweet, 1903-1906 (Madison, N.J.: Drew Theological Seminary).

40. William Warren Sweet, Jr., to James L. Ash, Jr., January 23, 1975; Esther Sweet Lewis to James L. Ash, Jr., February 23, 1975; Elizabeth Sweet Hix to James L. Ash, Jr., January 21, 1975.

41. William Warren Sweet, Jr., to James L. Ash, Jr., January 23, 1975; Esther Sweet Lewis to James L. Ash, Jr., February 23, 1975.

42. William Warren Sweet, "The Influence of the German Chorale upon Christian Music" (B.D. thesis, Drew Theological Seminary, 1906), pp. 1-3.

43. Irwin, "William Warren Sweet," p. 3; William Warren Sweet to William J. Thompson, January 20, 1931, William Warren Sweet Papers, Department of Special Collections, Regenstein Library, University of Chicago (hereafter cited as Sweet Papers UC), Box 2, Folder 9: ". . . Professor Rogers was, without any doubt in my mind my greatest teacher. . . . he gave me the first real glimpse of what scholarship meant and he inspired me with a desire to become a scholar."

44. Robert W. Rogers, *History of Babylonia and Assyria* (New York: Eaton & Mains, 1900).

45. The professor of history at Ohio Wesleyan during those years was Richard T. Stevenson, who received his doctorate from Ohio Wesleyan in 1938 (Hubbart, *Ohio Wesleyan's First Hundred Years*, p. 91; Junior Class of Ohio Wesleyan, *Bijou*, p. 11).

46. See John Higham, *History* (New York: Harper & Row, 1973), pp. 4, 92-103.

47. *Drew Year Book, 1904-1905*, p. 30.

48. "History, Economics, and Public Law," Columbia University Bulletin of Information, 5th ser., no. 10 (New York: Columbia University, 1905), p. 13; History Department Classbook, 1904-1922, Columbiana Collection, Low Memorial Library, Columbia University.

49. Harvey Wish, *The American Historian* (New York: Oxford University Press, 1960), p. 231.

50. William Warren Sweet, *American Culture and Religion* (Dallas: Southern Methodist University Press, 1951), p. 76. William Warren Sweet, *Methodism in American History*, 2d ed. (New York: Abingdon Press, 1953), p. 402.

51. William P. Tolley, ed., *Alumni Record of Drew Theological Seminary* (Madison, N.J.: Drew Theological Seminary, 1926), p. 363.

52. Peter N. VandenBerge, Director of Library Services, Ambrose Swasey Library, Colgate Rochester-Bexley Hall-Crozer Seminary, to James L. Ash, Jr., January 31, 1975.

53. William Warren Sweet, "Theories of the Atonement" (Th.M. thesis, Crozer Theological Seminary, 1907).

54. Official Transcript of William Warren Sweet, 1906-1912 (Philadelphia: University of Pennsylvania, Philosophy Department Records).

55. This date does not agree with some published data on Sweet which lists the date of his A.M. as 1907. My assumption is that the University of Pennsylvania records are accurate.

56. Official Transcript, University of Pennsylvania; interview with Paul R. Sweet.

57. Wish, *American Historian*, pp. 132-33.

58. William T. Hutchinson, "John Bach McMaster," in *The Marcus W. Jernegan Essays in American Historiography*, ed. William T. Hutchinson (Chicago: University of Chicago Press, 1937), p. 133.

59. Ibid., p. 132.

60. Herman V. Ames, *Proposed Amendments to the Constitution of the United States during the first century of its history*, American Historical Association Annual Report (Washington: Government Printing Office, 1897).

61. William Warren Sweet, *The Methodist Episcopal Church and the Civil War* (Cincinnati: Methodist Book Concern, 1912), p. 8.

62. Ibid., p. 62.

63. Ibid., pp. 179-80.

64. Ibid., p. 7.

65. Ibid., p. 87.

66. Sweet, *American Culture*, p. 72.

67. Ibid., p. 73.

68. C. R. Fish, review of *The Methodist Episcopal Church and the Civil War* by William Warren Sweet, in *American Historical Review* 18 (January 1913): 405-6.

69. J. H. Randall and G. Haines IV, "Controlling Assumptions in the Practice of Americans," in *Theory and Practice in Historical Study: A Report of the Committee on Historiography*, Social Science Research Council Bulletin no. 54 (New York, 1946).

70. Veysey, *Emergence of the American University*, p. 271.

71. Richard Hofstadter, *The Age of Reform* (New York: Random House, Vintage Books, 1955), p. 154; cf. Veysey, *Emergence of the American University*, p. 440: "The custodianship of popular values comprised the primary responsibility of the American university."

72. Cf. Martin E. Marty, *Righteous Empire* (New York: Dial Press, 1970); Robert T. Handy, *A Christian America* (London: Oxford University Press, 1971).

73. Hofstadter, *Age of Reform*, p. 204.

74. John Bach McMaster, quoted in Wish, *American Historian*, p. 137.

75. John Bach McMaster, *A History of the People of the United States*, 8 vols. (New York: Appleton, 1900), 5:159-60.

76. Hutchinson, "John Bach McMaster," p. 138.

77. Cf. infra, pp. 44-48, for a comparison of Sweet and Turner.

CHAPTER THREE

1. W. G. Hormell to President George R. Grose, DePauw University, August 13, 1913, Presidents' Files, DePauw University Archives, Greencastle, Indiana.

2. Richard T. Stevenson, Introduction to *The Methodist Episcopal Church and the Civil War* by William Warren Sweet, pp. 10-11.

3. *Ohio Wesleyan Transcript* 45 (May 23, 1912): 485.

4. Ibid. (June 10, 1913): 524.

5. Ibid.

6. Edwin H. Hughes to President George R. Grose, August 12, 1913, Presidents' Files, DePauw.

7. Edwin H. Hughes to President George R. Grose, August 13, 1913, Presidents' Files, DePauw.

8. Richard T. Stevenson to President George R. Grose, August 13, 1913, Presidents' Files, DePauw.

9. W. G. Hormell to President George R. Grose, August 13, 1913, Presidents' Files, DePauw.

10. T. G. Duvall to President George R. Grose, August 14, 1913, Presidents' Files, DePauw.

11. T. G. Duvall to President George R. Grose, August 19, 1913, Presidents' Files, DePauw.

12. William E. Smyser to President George R. Grose, August 14, 1913, Presidents' Files, DePauw.

13. President George R. Grose to Richard T. Stevenson, Vice President, Ohio Wesleyan University, August 15, 1913, Presidents' Files, DePauw.

14. William Warren Sweet to President George R. Grose, August 18, 1913, Presidents' Files, DePauw.

15. William Warren Sweet to President George R. Grose, August 18, 1913, Presidents' Files, DePauw.

16. Statement by Dr. H. A. Gobin, August 19, 1913, Presidents' Files, DePauw.

17. *Reports of the President and Other Officers of Ohio Wesleyan University for the College Year 1913-14* (Delaware, Ohio: Ohio Wesleyan, 1914), p. 6.

18. George B. Manhart, *DePauw through the Years*, 2 vols. (Greencastle, Ind.: DePauw University, 1962), 1:234.

19. "Asbury College of Liberal Arts," DePauw University Bulletin, pt. 1, 2d ser., no. 10 (Greencastle, Ind., 1913), pp. 65-67.

20. Manhart, *DePauw through the Years*, 1:234.

21. "College of Liberal Arts," DePauw University Bulletin, 3d ser., no. 1 (Greencastle, Ind., 1914), pp. 69-72.

22. "Asbury College of Liberal Arts," p. 67.

23. "College of Liberal Arts Annual Catalogue 1916-1917," DePauw University Bulletin, 3d ser., no. 4 (Greencastle, Ind., 1917), p. 81.

24. Junior Class of DePauw University, *The Mirage* (Greencastle, Ind.: DePauw University, 1916), p. 222.

25. William Warren Sweet, letter, April 9, 1918, Presidents' Files, DePauw.

26. President George R. Grose to William Warren Sweet, April 10, 1918, Presidents' Files, DePauw.

27. Elizabeth Sweet Hix to James L. Ash, Jr., January 21, 1975.

28. President George R. Grose to William Warren Sweet, June 9, 1916, Presidents' Files, DePauw.

29. Interview with Paul R. Sweet.

30. Paul R. Sweet to James L. Ash, Jr., January 28, 1975; Elizabeth Sweet Hix to James L. Ash, Jr., January 21, 1975.

31. *The Mirage*, p. 204.

32. Interview with Paul R. Sweet.

33. William Warren Sweet, "Methodist Church Influence in Southern Politics," *Mississippi Valley Historical Review* 1 (March 1915): 547.

34. Ibid.

35. Ibid.

36. See infra, pp. 77-82, 117-43.

37. Logan Esarey, review of *Circuit-Rider Days in Indiana* by William Warren Sweet, *Mississippi Valley Historical Review* 3 (September 1916): 250.

38. William Warren Sweet, *Circuit-Rider Days in Indiana* (Indianapolis, Ind.: W. K. Stewart, 1916), p. v.

39. Ibid., p. 31.

40. Ibid., pp. 31-32.

41. Ibid., p. 33.

42. Manhart, *DePauw through the Years*, 2: 493-94.

43. "Alumni News Letter," DePauw University Bulletin, 3d ser., no. 1 (Greencastle, Ind., 1914), p. 4.

44. James H. Timberlake, *Prohibition and the Progressive Movement* (Cambridge: Harvard University Press, 1966).

45. H. N. Herrick and William Warren Sweet, *A History of the North Indiana Conference of the Methodist Episcopal Church* (Indianapolis, Ind.: W. K. Steward, 1917), p. 221.

46. Andrew Sinclair, *Prohibition: The Era of Excess* (Boston: Little, Brown, 1962), pp. 9-22, 63-82; cf. Richard Hofstadter, *The Age of Reform* (New York: Random House, Vintage Books, 1955), p. 290: "[Prohibition] was carried about America by the rural-evangelical virus."

47. *New York Times*, January 5, 1959, p. 29.

48. William Warren Sweet, "The Indifference of Methodists to Their Past," *Zion's Herald*, May 14, 1919.

49. George H. Maxwell to William Warren Sweet, June 10, 1919, Sweet Papers UC, 1:13.

50. Frederick Jackson Turner, quoted in *The Turner Thesis*, ed. George R. Taylor, rev. ed. (Boston: D. C. Heath, 1956), p. x.

51. Frederick Jackson Turner, *The Frontier in American History* (New York: Henry Holt, 1920), p. 266.

52. Ibid., p. 293.

53. Ibid., p. 259.

54. Richard Hofstadter, "Turner and the Frontier Myth," *American Scholar* 18 (Autumn 1949), reprinted in *The Frontier Thesis*, ed. Ray A. Billington (New York: Holt, Rinehart & Winston, 1966), p. 102.

55. William Warren Sweet, *Circuit-Rider Days along the Ohio* (New York: Methodist Book Concern, 1923), p. 11.

56. Sweet, *The Rise of Methodism in the West* (New York: Methodist Book Concern, 1920), p. 58.

57. Ibid., p. 59.

58. Ibid., pp. 58-70.

59. William Warren Sweet, "Some Salient Characteristics of Frontier Religion," *Methodist Quarterly Review* 73 (July 1924): 452.

60. Sweet, *Rise of Methodism*, p. 62.

61. "The things typically American today, whether in politics or religion, have been largely the product of frontier influences" (William Warren Sweet, "Some Significant Factors in American Church History," *Journal of Religion* 7 [January 1927]: 11).

62. William Warren Sweet, *Religion in the Development of American Culture 1785-1840* (New York: Charles Scribner's Sons, 1952), pp. 312-14.

63. Turner, *The Frontier in American History*, p. 1.

64. Sweet, *Rise of Methodism*, p. 22.
65. Ibid., p. 59.
66. Ibid., p. 14.
67. William Warren Sweet, *The Story of Religions in America*, 1st ed. (New York: Harper & Bros., 1930), p. 316.
68. Sweet, "Salient Characteristics of Frontier Religion," pp. 437-38.
69. Turner, *The Frontier in American History*, p. 35.
70. William Warren Sweet, "The Frontier in American Christianity," in *Environmental Factors in Christian History*, ed. John T. McNeill et al. (Chicago: University of Chicago Press, 1939), p. 390.
71. Sweet, "Salient Characteristics of Frontier Religion," p. 439.
72. Ibid., p. 452.
73. Ibid., p. 440.
74. Ibid.
75. William Warren Sweet, *Our American Churches* (New York: Methodist Book Concern, 1924), p. 9.
76. Ibid., p. 38.
77. Ibid., p. 98.
78. Ibid., p. 107.
79. Ibid., p. 60.
80. Ibid., p. 74.
81. Ibid., p. 79.
82. Ibid., p. 65.
83. Ibid., pp. 67-68.
84. Ibid., p. 68.
85. Ibid., p. 87.
86. Ibid., p. 86.
87. William Warren Sweet, *Greencastle: A Hundred Years' View, 1823-1923* (Greencastle, Ind.: Central National Bank, 1923).
88. William Warren Sweet and George B. Manhart, *History: A Survey* (n.p.: American College Society, 1923).
89. William R. Shepherd, review of *A History of Latin America* by William Warren Sweet, *American Historical Review* 24 (July 1919): 742; Sweet replied to these criticisms by venerating the function of the skillful general historian over the specialist in the writing of elementary texts (Hutton Webster, review of Sweet, *History of Latin America*, in *Mississippi Valley Historical Review* 12 [December 1925]: 446-47); later he replied to the same kind of criticism by charging, "The book has always been resented by some of the little group who call themselves Latin American specialists . . ." (William Warren Sweet to John W. Langdale, May 12, 1930, Sweet Papers UC, 1:2).
90. Shepherd, review of *History of Latin America* by Sweet, p. 741.
91. Oscar Handlin, *Race and Nationality in American Life* (Boston: Little, Brown, 1957), pp. 176-77; Barbara M. Soloman, *Ancestors and Immigrants* (Chicago: University of Chicago Press, Phoenix Books, 1972), p. 195-209; Edward N. Saveth, *American Historians and European Immigrants 1875-1925* (New York: Russell & Russell, 1965); John Higham, *Strangers in the Land* (New Brunswick, N.J.: Rutgers University Press, 1955).
92. Handlin, *Race and Nationality*, p. 96.
93. Sweet, *A History of Latin America* (New York: Abingdon Press, 1919), p. 7.
94. Ibid.
95. Ibid., p. 222.

96. Ibid., p. 221.

97. Ibid., pp. 223-24.

98. Ibid., pp. 232, 236.

99. Madison Grant, *The Passing of the Great Race* (New York: Charles Scribner, 1916); Henry P. Fairchild, *The Melting-Pot Mistake* (Boston: Little, Brown, 1926).

100. Sweet, *The Story of Religions in America*, 1st ed., pp. 510-11.

101. William Warren Sweet, review of *The United States and Civilization* by John U. Nef, *Mississippi Valley Historical Review* 29 (June 1942): 119.

102. Sweet, *History of Latin America*, pp. 224-25.

103. Edward Hislop to President George R. Grose, March 10, 1919, Presidents' Files, DePauw.

104. Benson Baker to President George R. Grose, March 9, 1922, Presidents' Files, DePauw.

105. William Warren Sweet to Roy O. West, July 16, 1923, Presidents' Files, DePauw.

106. William Warren Sweet, "Every Dog Has His Day and I've Had Mine," *Divinity School News* 13 (August 1, 1946): 4-5.

107. Ibid., p. 6.

CHAPTER FOUR

1. William W. Sweet, Jr., to James L. Ash, Jr., January 23, 1975.

2. William Warren Sweet, "Every Dog Has His Day and I've Had Mine," *Divinity School News* 13 (August 1, 1946): 5-6.

3. Shirley Jackson Case to William Warren Sweet, November 10, 1934, Sweet Papers UC, 1:5; President George R. Grose to William Warren Sweet, June 9, 1923, Presidents' Files, DePauw.

4. William W. Sweet, Jr., to James L. Ash, Jr., January 23, 1975.

5. Harold McNeill, "William Warren Sweet," essay based on an interview with William W. Sweet, Jr., held on November 10, 1971, in Fort Worth, Texas, p. 3.

6. William W. Sweet, Jr., to James L. Ash, Jr., January 23, 1975.

7. More than once he wrote the Methodist bishop a request to give the church a minister who would appeal more to students and faculty of the university (see for example William Warren Sweet to Bishop E. L. Waldorf, n.d., Sweet Papers UC, 2:12).

8. William K. Anderson to William Warren Sweet, September 27, 1941, Sweet Papers UC, 1:1.

9. William W. Sweet, Jr., to James L. Ash, Jr., January 23, 1975.

10. James H. Robinson, "Sacred and Profane History," in *Annual Report of the American Historical Association for the Year 1899*, 2 vols. (Washington: Government Printing Office, 1900), 1:533, quoted in William F. Riley, Jr., "The Influence of Turner's Frontier Thesis upon American Religious Historiography" (M.A. thesis, Western Kentucky University, 1974), p. 15.

11. George J. Bayles, "American Ecclesiology," in *Annual Report of the American Historical Association for the Year 1900*, 2 vols. (Washington: Government Printing Office, 1901), 1:129-38.

12. See the Appendix entitled "The American Society of Church History," in *Church History in the Age of Science*, by Henry W. Bowden (Chapel Hill: University of North Carolina Press, 1971), pp. 239-45.

13. Simeon E. Baldwin, "Religion Still the Key to History," *American Historical Review* 12 (January 1907): 219-43.

14. J. Franklin Jameson, "The American Acta Sanctorum," *American Historical Review* 13 (January 1908): 298.

15. Ibid., p. 302.

16. Francis A. Christie, "Report of the Conference on the Teaching of Church History," in *Annual Report of the American Historical Association for the Year 1904* (Washington: Government Printing Office, 1905), p. 216.

17. Floyd W. Reeves, "Scholarly Reputation," in *The University of Chicago Survey*, 12 vols. (Chicago: University of Chicago Press, 1933), 3:39-54.

18. Shailer Mathews, *The Spiritual Interpretation of History*, 2d ed. (Cambridge: Harvard University Press, 1920), p. 68.

19. Ibid., p. ix.

20. Ibid.

21. See Stephen Wurster, "The Modernism of Shailer Mathews: A Study in American Religious Progressivism" (Ph.D. diss., University of Iowa, 1972).

22. See Archie H. Jones, "American Protestantism and the Science of History" (Ph.D. diss., University of Chicago, 1954), pp. 6-40; William J. Hynes, *Shirley Jackson Case and the Chicago School* (Chico, Calif.: Scholars Press, 1981).

23. Jones, "American Protestantism," p. 24.

24. Ibid.

25. Bowden, *Church History in the Age of Science*.

26. Jones, "American Protestantism," pp. 14-16.

27. Mathews, *Spiritual Interpretation of History*, p. vii: "Democracy . . . has been disclosed as an irrepressible tendency"; see also Shailer Mathews, *Patriotism and Religion* (New York: Macmillan, 1918); Andrew C. McLaughlin, "American History and American Democracy," *American Historical Review* 20 (1915): 256-70.

28. Peter G. Mode, "The Influence of the Black Death on the English Monasteries" (Ph.D. diss., University of Chicago, 1916).

29. "The Divinity School 1916-1917," *University of Chicago Circular of Information* 17 (February 1917): 65-67; "The Divinity School 1921-1922," *University of Chicago Circular of Information* 21 (February 1921): 66-70; "The Divinity School 1925-26," *University of Chicago Announcements* 25 (January 1925): 58-62.

30. Peter G. Mode, *Source Book and Bibliographical Guide for American Church History* (Menasha, Wis.: George Banta, 1921).

31. Peter G. Mode, *The Frontier Spirit in American Christianity* (New York: Macmillan, 1923).

32. "The Divinity School 1916-1917," p. 67.

33. Mode, *Frontier Spirit*, p. ix.

34. Ibid., p. 14.

35. Ibid., p. x.

36. Shirley Jackson Case, "The Historical Study of Religion," *Journal of Religion* 1 (1921): 1-17.

37. John Higham, *History* (New York: Harper & Row, 1973), p. 99.

38. James H. Robinson, *The New History* (New York: Macmillan, 1912); see also Higham, *History*, pp. 104-16.

39. Case, "Historical Study of Religion," p. 17.

40. Shirley Jackson Case, *The Christian Philosophy of History* (Chicago: University of Chicago Press, 1943), p. 131, quoted in Jones, "American Protestantism," p. 105.

41. Shirley Jackson Case to President E. D. Burton, October 22, 1923, The Presidents' Papers, ca. 1925-45, box 111, folder 1, Department of Special Collections, Regenstein Library, University of Chicago.

42. *School and Society* 22 (August 1, 1925): 137.

43. Joseph W. Mauck to Peter G. Mode, June 25, 1926, Sweet Papers UC, 1:13.

44. See Shirley Jackson Case, *The Evolution of Early Christianity: A Genetic Study of First Century Christianity in Relation to Its Religious Environment* (Chicago: University of Chicago Press, 1914); Shirley Jackson Case, *The Social Origins of Christianity* (Chicago: University of Chicago Press, 1923); Hynes, *Shirley Jackson Case.*

45. Louis B. Jennings, *The Bibliography and Biography of Shirley Jackson Case* (Chicago: University of Chicago Press, 1949), p. 32.

46. For an example of the distinctive emphases of Case's department see his festschrift: John T. McNeill, Matthew Spinka, and Harold R. Willoughby, eds., *Environmental Factors in Christian History* (Chicago: University of Chicago Press, 1939).

47. See Jones, "American Protestantism," pp. 25-26.

48. Jennings, *Biography of Shirley Jackson Case*, p. 33.

49. Shirley Jackson Case, Matthew Spinka, and William Warren Sweet to Waldo G. Leland, May 19, 1933, Sweet Papers UC, 1:1.

50. Shirley Jackson Case to William Warren Sweet, December 16, 1932, Sweet Papers, UC, 1:5.

51. Shirley Jackson Case to William Warren Sweet, December 2, 1932, Sweet Papers UC, 1:5.

52. Jennings, *Biography of Shirley Jackson Case*, p. 33.

53. William Warren Sweet to Rev. D. A. Abbott, October 15, 1927, Sweet Papers UC, 1:1.

54. William Warren Sweet, "Annual Report of the Research Institute in the Department of Church History, July 1927 to July 1928," Presidents' Papers, ca. 1925-45, box 111, folder 1, Department of Special Collections, Regenstein Library, University of Chicago.

55. William Warren Sweet to Rev. S. G. Ayres, January 6, 1928, Sweet Papers UC, 1:1.

56. Shailer Mathews to William Warren Sweet, July 9, 1929, Sweet Papers UC, 1:15.

57. Shirley Jackson Case to Gilbert Loveland, April 4, 1930, Sweet Papers UC, 1:9.

58. Shirley Jackson Case, Introduction to William Warren Sweet, *Religion on the American Frontier*, vol. 1: *The Baptists 1783-1830* (New York: Henry Holt, 1931), p. vi.

59. Ibid.

60. Gilbert Loveland to William Warren Sweet, June 23, 1936, Sweet Papers UC, 1:9.

61. William Warren Sweet to E. P. Cheyney, July 10, 1934, Sweet Papers UC, 1:4.

62. Robert S. Fletcher, review of *The Congregationalists*, vol. 3 of *Religion on the American Frontier* by William Warren Sweet, *Mississippi Valley Historical Review* 26 (March 1940): 570.

63. William Warren Sweet, *Religion in the Development of American Culture 1785-1840* (New York: Charles Scribner's Sons, 1952), p. 313.

64. Daniel Dorchester, *Christianity in the United States from the First Settlement Down to the Present Time* (New York: Phillips & Hunt, 1888).

65. William Warren Sweet, *Methodism in American History*, 1st ed. (New York: Methodist Book Concern, 1933), p. 143.

66. William Warren Sweet, *Religion on the American Frontier*, vol. 4: *The Methodists* (Chicago: University of Chicago Press, 1946), p. 42.

67. Sweet, *Methodism in American History*, 1st ed., p. 144.

68. William Warren Sweet, *The Story of Religions in America*, 1st ed. (New York: Harper & Bros., 1930), p. 280.

69. Ibid., p. 317; cf. supra, p. 75; Sweet, *Methodism in American History*, 1st ed., p. 149.

70. William Warren Sweet, *Revivalism in America* (New York: Charles Scribner, 1944), p. 128.

71. Ibid., p. 140.

72. Ibid., p. 129.

73. Sweet, *The Baptists*, p. 55.

74. Sweet, *The Story of Religions in America*, 1st ed., p. 370; cf. Sweet, *The Baptists*, "The Rise of the Anti-Mission Baptists," pp. 58-76.

75. Sweet, *Religion in the Development of American Culture*, p. 110.

76. Herbert Gambrell to James L. Ash, Jr., October 18, 1974.

77. Sweet, *The Methodists*, p. 51.

78. William Warren Sweet, *Religion on the American Frontier*, vol. 2: *The Presbyterians* (New York: Harper & Bros., 1936), p. 23.

79. Sweet, *The Story of Religions in America*, 1st ed., p. 214.

80. William Warren Sweet, *The Congregationalists*, p. 11.

81. Ibid.

82. Sweet, *The Story of Religions in America*, 1st ed., p. 296.

83. Sweet, *Religion in the Development of American Culture*, p. 100.

84. E.g., "The Methodist system functioned effectively, not so much because of its mechanical perfection, but rather because of the self-sacrificing devotion of the circuit riders, who, like Paul, counted not their lives dear unto themselves" (Sweet, *The Methodists*, p. 50).

85. William Warren Sweet, *The Story of Religion in America*, 3d ed. (New York: Harper & Bros., 1950), pp. 214-15; the final sentence is contained only in the third edition.

86. Sweet, *The Story of Religions in America*, 1st ed., p. 59.

87. Sidney E. Mead, "Professor Sweet's Religion and Culture in America," *Church History* 22 (March 1953): 35.

88. See Sweet, *The Story of Religions in America*, 1st ed., pp. 298-321; Sweet, *Religion in the Development of American Culture*, pp. 2-53.

89. That Sweet believed he was tracing the history of a single entity called American religion is clear from the fact that in response to criticism he dropped the "s" from "Religions" in the second and third editions of *The Story of Religions in America* (see A. W. Drury to William Warren Sweet, November 14, 1930, Sweet Papers UC, 1:6).

90. William Warren Sweet, "Some Significant Factors in American Church History," *Journal of Religion* 7 (1927): 1-15.

91. Sweet, *The Story of Religions in America*, 1st ed., p. 447.

92. Ibid., p. 225.

93. Sweet, *The Congregationalists*, p. 43.

94. William Warren Sweet, *The American Churches: An Interpretation* (London: Epworth Press, 1947), p. 49.

95. Winfred E. Garrison, quoted in Sweet, *American Churches*, p. 51.
96. Ibid., p. 53.
97. Ibid., p. 66.
98. Sweet, "The Frontier in American Christianity," p. 391.
99. Sweet, "Significant Factors in American Church History," p. 15.
100. Sweet, *The Story of Religions in America*, 1st ed., p. 1.
101. Ibid., p. 411.
102. Ibid., p. 503.
103. Sweet, *The American Churches*, p. 32.
104. Daryl Chase to William Warren Sweet, September 29, 1938, Sweet Papers UC, 1:4.
105. Sweet, *Revivalism in America*, p. xiii.
106. Sweet, *Religion in the Development of American Culture*, p. 153.
107. Sweet, *The Story of Religions in America*, 1st ed., p. 396.
108. Sweet, *Revivalism in America*, pp. 164-65, 94.
109. Sweet, *The Story of Religions in America*, 1st ed., pp. 401-11.
110. Sweet, *Revivalism in America*, p. 176; Sweet further admits that these groups may be the location of much religious genius: "it is 'the cranks' which turn the world" (ibid., p. 177); cf. Sweet, *The American Churches*, p. 25.
111. Robert Baird, *Religion in America*, ed. Henry W. Bowden (New York: Harper & Row, 1970), pp. 210, 257.
112. Ibid., p. 276.
113. Ibid.
114. Ibid., p. 280.
115. Dorchester, *Christianity in the United States*, p. 775.
116. Ibid., p. 780.
117. Ibid.
118. Leonard W. Bacon, *A History of American Christianity* (New York: Charles Scribner, 1901), p. 397.
119. Ibid., p. 335.
120. Ibid.
121. Ibid., p. 268.
122. Henry K. Rowe, *The History of Religion in the United States* (New York: Macmillan, 1924), pp. 86-87, 176-77.
123. Ibid., p. 84.
124. Ibid., p. 119.
125. Ibid., p. 205.
126. Ibid., p. 117.
127. Ibid., p. 188.
128. Martin E. Marty, "The American Mainstream: Generalizations about the Protestant Denominations in the General Histories of American Christianity," typewritten (Chicago, 1956).
129. Ibid., p. 35.
130. Marty, *Righteous Empire* (New York: Dial Press, 1970), pp. 199-209; Robert T. Handy, *A Christian America* (London: Oxford University Press, 1971), pp. 117-213.
131. Sweet approached the Charles Scribner publishing house in September, 1927, asking if the company was interested in publishing his proposed "History of American Christianity" (W. D. Howe to William Warren Sweet, September 30, 1927, Sweet Papers UC, 2:5).
132. "The Divinity School 1927-1928," *University of Chicago Announcements* 27 (February 1927): 60.

133. Frederick C. Macmillan to William Warren Sweet, October 13, 1931, Sweet Papers UC, 1:13.

134. William A. Irwin, "William Warren Sweet" (eulogy delivered at Sweet's funeral in Dallas, 1959), p. 6.

135. *Chicago Tribune*, March 9, 1930.

136. Elizabeth Sweet Hix to James L. Ash, Jr.

137. Eugene Exman to William Warren Sweet, July 27, 1928, Sweet Papers UC, 1:10.

138. Eugene Exman to William Warren Sweet, December 12, 1928, Sweet Papers UC, 1:10.

139. William Warren Sweet to Eugene Exman, March 25, 1929, Sweet Papers UC, 1:10.

140. Eugene Exman to William Warren Sweet, April 7, 1930, Sweet Papers UC, 1:10.

141. William Warren Sweet, synopsis of *The Story of Religions in America*, April 1930, Sweet Papers UC, 1:10.

142. W. M. Gewehr, review of *The Story of Religions in America* in *American Historical Review* 37 (January 1932): 349.

143. Winfred E. Garrison, review of *The Story of Religions in America* in *Christian Century* 47 (December 31, 1930): 1627.

144. Publication and sales records for *The Story of Religions in America*, Harper & Row, New York.

145. William Warren Sweet to Shirley Jackson Case, July 24, 1931, Sweet Papers UC, 1:5.

146. Matthew Spinka to William Warren Sweet, October 13, 1932, Sweet Papers UC, 2:5.

147. Arthur C. McGiffert, Jr., to William Warren Sweet, November 15, 1932, Sweet Papers UC, 1:13.

148. William Warren Sweet to Shirley Jackson Case, October 10, 1932, Sweet Papers UC, 1:5.

149. R. G. McCutchan to William Warren Sweet, November 10, 1932, Sweet Papers UC, 1:13.

150. William Warren Sweet to Shirley Jackson Case, July 24, 1931, Sweet Papers UC, 1:5.

151. Lynn Harold Hough to William Warren Sweet, December 21, 1934, Sweet Papers UC, 1:9.

152. Shirley Jackson Case to William Warren Sweet, November 10, 1934, Sweet Papers UC, 1:9.

153. Shirley Jackson Case to William Warren Sweet, January 9, 1935, Sweet Papers UC, 1:9.

154. William Warren Sweet to Lynn Harold Hough, January 11, 1935, Sweet Papers UC, 1:9.

155. John W. Langdale to William Warren Sweet, March 19, 1932, Sweet Papers UC, 1:2.

156. Sweet, *Methodism in American History*, 1st ed.

157. William Warren Sweet, "Methodist Unification," in *American Culture and Religion* (Dallas, Southern Methodist University Press, 1951), p. 76.

158. Ibid., p. 74.

159. *Journal of the Uniting Conference of the Methodist Church* (New York: Methodist Publishing House, 1939), p. 95.

160. Ibid., p. 396.

161. William Warren Sweet, "The Frontier in American Christianity," in

John T. McNeill et al., eds., *Environmental Factors in Christian History* (Chicago: University of Chicago Press, 1939), p. 398.

162. Shirley Jackson Case to William Warren Sweet, November 10, 1934, Sweet Papers UC, 1:9.

163. Winthrop S. Hudson to James L. Ash, Jr., June 5, 1974.

164. "Minutes of the Twenty-seventh Annual Meeting of the Mississippi Valley Historical Association," *Mississippi Valley Historical Review* 21 (September 1934): 213-14.

165. Allan MacRossie to William Warren Sweet, January 8, 1935, Sweet Papers UC, 1:13.

166. Edwin S. Gaustad, "Religion in America: History and Historiography," American Historical Association Pamphlet 260 (Washington, D.C.: American Historical Association, 1973), p. 52.

167. Perhaps it was his use of multiple student assistants which led to the inclusion of a plagiarized passage in the introduction to his volume of Congregationalist sources. Pages 6-7 contain a brief section identical to material in a Yale dissertation which was later published with an editorial note accusing Sweet of the error. Sweet was very embarrassed by the incident and took complete responsibility for it, stating that his notes must have gotten mixed up (William Warren Sweet to Bernhard Knollenberg, October 14, 1941, Sweet Papers UC, 1:10). Similar charges were made concerning two of Sweet's DePauw publications (Isaac J. Cox, review of *A History of Latin America* by William Warren Sweet, in *Mississippi Valley Historical Review* 6 [December 1919]: 435; C. B. Swaney, review of *Circuit-Rider Days along the Ohio* by William Warren Sweet, in *Mississippi Valley Historical Review* 10 [December 1923]: 339). These instances were probably unintentional and accidental.

168. Shirley Jackson Case to William Warren Sweet, October 14, 1932, Sweet Papers UC, 1:5.

169. John W. Langdale to Rev. W. L. Duren, February 26, 1934, Sweet Papers UC, 1:2.

170. Harvey Wish, review of *Religion in the Development of American Culture* by William Warren Sweet, in *American Historical Review* 59 (October 1953): 138.

171. Willard L. Sperry to William Warren Sweet, June 3, 1943, Sweet Papers UC, 2:7; Case responded to this news with the comment: "I was much interested to learn about your invitation to teach at Harvard next year. It must be that Harvard is waking up to the task of modern education. I did not suppose that it would be interested in anything so recent as American Church History." Shirley Jackson Case to William Warren Sweet, September 30, 1943, Sweet Papers UC, 1:5.

172. Willard L. Sperry to William Warren Sweet, November 16, 1945, Sweet Papers UC, 2:7.

173. William Warren Sweet, *Religion in Colonial America* (New York: Charles Scribner, 1942).

174. Curtis Nettels, review of *Religion in Colonial America* by Sweet, *Mississippi Valley Historical Review* 29 (December 1942): 441; Raymond P. Stearns, review of *Religion in Colonial America* by Sweet, *American Historical Review* 49 (April 1944): 490.

175. Sweet, *Revivalism in America*.

176. William Warren Sweet to Shirley Jackson Case, October 18, 1944, Sweet Papers UC, 1:5.

177. William Warren Sweet to Willard L. Sperry, May 31, 1945, Sweet Papers UC, 2:7.
178. Willard L. Sperry to William Warren Sweet, June 20, 1945, Sweet Papers UC, 2:7.
179. William Warren Sweet to Eugene A. Tilleux, March 6, 1946, Sweet Papers UC, 2:10.
180. Cf. supra, pp. 53-55.
181. William Warren Sweet, "Cultural Pluralism in the American Tradition," *Christendom* 11 (1946): 316.
182. Ibid.
183. Ibid., p. 503.
184. Ibid., p. 508.
185. William Warren Sweet, review of *The Schism in the Methodist Episcopal Church* by John N. Norwood, *American Historical Review* 29 (January 1924): 351.
186. William Warren Sweet, review of *The History of Religion in the United States*, by Henry K. Rowe, in *Mississippi Valley Historical Review* 12 (September 1925): 281.
187. William Warren Sweet, "Some Religious Aspects of the Kansas Struggle," *Journal of Religion* 7 (October 1927): 578.
188. Sweet, "Significant Factors in American Church History," p. 4.
189. Ray A. Billington to William Warren Sweet, December 30, 1935, Sweet Papers UC, 1:3.
190. Sidney E. Mead, "Professor Sweet's Religion and Culture in America," *Church History* 22 (March 1953): 34.
191. Sweet, "Every Dog Has His Day," p. 6.
192. Wish, review of *Religion in the Development of American Culture*, p. 140.

CHAPTER FIVE

1. The full text of the speech is reprinted as Appendix A.
2. William Warren Sweet, "Every Dog Has His Day and I've Had Mine," *Divinity School News* 13 (August 1, 1946): 7-8.
3. Shirley Jackson Case to William Warren Sweet, June 18, 1947, William Warren Sweet Papers, Bridwell Library, Southern Methodist University (hereafter cited as Sweet Papers SMU), Box 1, Folder 14.
4. William Warren Sweet to James R. Joy, October 23, 1947, Methodist Historical Collection, Rose Memorial Library, Drew University, Madison, N.J.
5. Kenneth S. Latourette, review of *The American Churches: An Interpretation* (London: Epworth Press, 1947), by William Warren Sweet, in *Mississippi Valley Historical Review* 35 (December 1948): 535-36.
6. Willard L. Sperry to William Warren Sweet, n.d., Sweet Papers UC, 2:7; see Willard L. Sperry, *Religion in America* (Cambridge: Cambridge University Press, 1946; New York: Macmillan, 1946).
7. John R. Bodo, *The Protestant Clergy and Public Issues 1812-1848* (Princeton: Princeton University Press, 1954), p. 188.
8. Cf. supra, p. 96.
9. William A. Irwin, "William Warren Sweet" (eulogy delivered at Sweet's funeral in Dallas, 1959), p. 6.
10. Herbert Gambrell to James L. Ash, Jr.
11. William Warren Sweet to Eugene B. Hawk, June 24, 1949, Deans' Files, Perkins School of Theology, Southern Methodist University, Dallas, Texas.

12. Herbert Gambrell to James L. Ash, Jr.
13. William Warren Sweet to Umphrey Lee, March 12, 1948, Sweet Papers SMU, 2:6.
14. Memorandum of agreement between Eugene B. Hawk and Umphrey Lee, n.d., Sweet Papers SMU, 2:6; see also William Warren Sweet to Eugene B. Hawk, June 24, 1949, Deans' Files, Perkins School of Theology, Souhern Methodist University.
15. William Warren Sweet to Merrimon Cuninggim, February 9, 1951, Deans' Files, Perkins School of Theology.
16. William Warren Sweet to Edwin E. Aubrey, December 5, 1950, Sweet Papers SMU, 1:3.
17. William Warren Sweet to Merrimon Cuninggim, March 18, 1951, Deans' Files, Perkins School of Theology.
18. William Warren Sweet to Merrimon Cuninggim, February 9, 1951, Deans' Files, Perkins School of Theology.
19. William Warren Sweet to Edwin E. Aubrey, December 5, 1950, Sweet Papers SMU, 1:3.
20. Merrimon Cuninggim to William Warren Sweet, June 11, 1952, Deans' Files, Perkins School of Theology.
21. Herbert Gambrell to James L. Ash, Jr.
22. J. Franklin Jameson, "The American Acta Sanctorum," quoted in William Warren Sweet, *Religion in the Development of American Culture 1785-1840* (New York: Charles Scribner's Sons, 1952), p. vii.
23. Whitney R. Cross, *The Burned-Over District: The Social and Intellectual History of Enthusiastic Religion in Western New York, 1800-1850* (New York: Cornell University Press, 1950).
24. Sidney E. Mead, "Professor Sweet's Religion and Culture in America," *Church History* 22 (March 1953): 33-49.
25. H. Shelton Smith, review of *Religion in the Development of American Culture*, in *Theology Today* 10 (January 1954): 561-64.
26. Cf. supra, pp. 44-48.
27. Winthrop S. Hudson, review of *Religion in the Development of American Culture*, in *Journal of Bible and Religion* 22 (January 1954): 49.
28. William Warren Sweet, *Virginia Methodism: A History* (Richmond, Va.: Whittet & Shepperson, 1955).
29. Herbert Gambrell to James L. Ash, Jr.
30. William W. Sweet, Jr., to James L. Ash, Jr., August 13, 1975.
31. William Warren Sweet to William W. Sweet, Jr., August 19, 1958, Sweet Papers SMU, 2:28.
32. William W. Sweet, Jr., to James L. Ash, Jr., August 13, 1975.
33. Jaroslav Pelikan, "Methodism's Contribution to America," in *The History of American Methodism*, ed. Emory S. Bucke, 3 vols. (New York: Abingdon Press, 1964), 3:597.

Bibliography

BOOKS BY WILLIAM WARREN SWEET

The American Churches: An Interpretation. London: Epworth Press, 1947.

American Culture and Religion. Dallas: Southern Methodist University Press, 1951.

Greencastle: A Hundred Years' View, 1823-1923. Greencastle, Ind.: Central National Bank, 1923.

A History of Latin America. New York: Abingdon Press, 1919, 1929.

Indiana Asbury—DePauw University, 1837-1937. New York: Abingdon Press, 1937.

Makers of Christianity: From John Cotton to Lyman Abbott. New York: Henry Holt, 1937.

Men of Zeal: The Romance of American Methodist Beginnings. New York: Abingdon Press, 1935.

Methodism in American History. New York: Methodist Book Concern, 1933, 1954.

The Methodist Episcopal Church and the Civil War. Cincinnati: Methodist Book Concern, 1912.

Our American Churches. New York: Methodist Book Concern, 1924.

Religion in Colonial America. New York: Charles Scribner, 1942.

Religion in the Development of American Culture, 1765-1840. New York: Charles Scribner's Sons, 1952.

Revivalism in America. New York: Charles Scribner, 1944.

The Story of Religions in America. New York: Harper & Bros., 1930, 1939, 1950.

Virginia Methodism: A History. Richmond, Va.: Whittet & Shepperson, 1955.

With LEE, UMPHREY. *A Short History of Methodism.* Nashville: Abingdon Press, 1956.

With MANHART, GEORGE B. *History: A Survey.* N.p.: American Col[lege] Society, 1923.

BOOKS EDITED BY WILLIAM WARREN SWEET

Circuit-Rider Days along the Ohio. Cincinnati: Methodist Book Concern, 1923.

Circuit-Rider Days in Indiana. Indianapolis: W. K. Stewart, 1916.

Religion on the American Frontier, vol. 1: *The Baptists, 1783-1830.* New York: Henry Holt, 1931.

Religion on the American Frontier, vol. 2: *The Presbyterians, 1783-1840.* New York: Harper & Bros., 1936.

Religion on the American Frontier, vol. 3: *The Congregationalists, 1783-1850.* Chicago: University of Chicago Press, 1939.

Religion on the American Frontier, vol. 4: *The Methodists, 1783-1840.* Chicago: University of Chicago Press, 1946.

The Rise of Methodism in the West. New York: Methodist Book Concern, 1920.

With HERRICK, HORACE N. *A History of the North Indiana Conference of the Methodist Episcopal Church.* Indianapolis: W. K. Stewart, 1917.

ARTICLES AND ESSAYS BY WILLIAM WARREN SWEET

"The American Colonial Environment and Religious Liberty." *Church History* 4 (1935): 43-56.

"Christianity in the Americas." In *A Bibliographical Guide to the History of Christianity,* edited by Shirley Jackson Case. Chicago: University of Chicago Press, 1931.

"Christianity in the Americas." In *A Short History of Christianity,* edited by Archibald C. Baker. Chicago: University of Chicago Press, 1940.

"Church and State." In *Building a Moral Reserve: Or the Civic Respon-*

sibilities of the Christian Citizen, edited by Shirley Jackson Case.
Chicago: American Institute of Sacred Literature, 1930.
"Church Archives in the United States." *Church History* 8 (1939): 43-53.
"The Churches as Moral Courts of the Frontier." *Church History* 2
(1933): 3-21.
"The Civilizing Influence of the Medieval Church." *Bibliotheca Sacra* 71
(1914): 458-65.
"The Coming of the Circuit Rider across the Mountains." *Mississippi
Valley Historical Review* 5 (1918): 271-82.
"The Cultural and Educational Influence of the Frontier Churches."
Mississippi Valley Historical Review 25 (1938): 243-44.
"Cultural Pluralism in the American Tradition." *Christendom* 11 (1946):
316-26, 501-8.
"DePauw, Washington Charles." *DAB* 5:244.*
"The Development of Religious Liberty in Colonial America." *American
Historical Review* 40 (1935): 435-45.
"The English Bible in the Making of America." *Southern Workman* 64
(1935): 341-45.
"Every Dog Has His Day and I've Had Mine." [University of Chicago]
Divinity School News 13 (1946): 4-8.
"The First Circuit Riders of the West." *Methodist Review* 100 (1917):
563.
[A Five Hundred Word History of the United States.] *Chicago Tribune,*
March 9, 1930.
"The Frontier in American Christianity." In *Environmental Factors in
Christian History,* edited by John T. McNeill, Matthew Spinka, and
Harold R. Willoughby. Chicago: University of Chicago Press, 1939.
"Gray, Isaac Pusey." *DAB* 7:519-20.
"Grose, William." *DAB* 8:16.
"Henderson, Charles Richmond." *DAB* 8:524-25.
"Hovey, Alvin Peterson." *DAB* 9:270-71.
"Howard, Timothy Edward." *DAB* 9:281-82.
"The Indifference of Methodists to Their Past." *Zion's Herald,* May 14,
1919.
"John Wesley and Scientific Discovery." *Christian Century* 40 (1923):
591-92.

---

* The abbreviation *DAB,* for *Dictionary of American Biography,* ed. Allan
Johnson (New York: Scribner, 1943), is used in this and subsequent sections.

"John Wesley in Ireland." *Methodist Review* 106 (1923): 380-91.

"John Wesley, Tory." *American Historical Review* 26 (1921): 427-40.

"Larrabee, William Clark." *DAB* 11:7.

"McCaine, Alexander." *DAB* 11:560.

"Methodist Church Influence in Southern Politics." *Mississippi Valley Historical Review* 1 (1915): 545-60.

"The Methodist Episcopal Church and Reconstruction." *Journal of the Illinois State Historical Society* 7 (1914): 147-65.

"Methodist Principles and Community Religion." In *Community Religion and the Denominational Heritage*, edited by J. R. Hargreaves. New York: Harper & Bros., 1930.

"Nast, William." *DAB* 12:393.

"Negro Churches in the South: A Phase of Reconstruction." *Methodist Review* 104 (1921): 405-18.

"Nevin, John Williamson." *DAB* 12:442-43.

"Pennsylvania Men and the Church." [University of Pennsylvania Alumni Society] *General Magazine and Historical Chronicle*, April 1942, pp. 348-57.

"Pertinent Fields of Research in Colleges." *American Historical Review* 30 (1925): 458-60.

"The Protestant Churches." *Annals of the American Academy of Political and Social Science* 256 (1948): 43-52.

"Quale, William Alfred." *DAB* 15:298.

"The Rapprochement in American Protestantism." *Religion in Life* 11 (1941-42): 74-83.

"Religion and the Westward March." *Ohio Archeological and Historical Quarterly* 50 (1941): 71-83.

"Religion in Our School Histories." *Christian Century* 41 (1924): 1502-4.

"Religious Enthusiasm as a Motive-force in Spanish Colonization." *Methodist Review* 111 (1928): 569-80.

"Religious Revivals." *Encyclopedia Britannica*, 14th ed., 19:240-41.

"The Rise of the Anti-Mission Baptists." *Methodist Review* 112 (1929): 650-65.

"The Rise of Theological Schools in America." *Church History* 6 (1937): 260-74.

"Scott, Orange." *DAB* 16:497-98.

"Shinn, Asa." *DAB* 17:110-11.

"Snethen, Nicholas." *DAB* 17:382-83.

"Some Present Day Latin-American Problems." *Methodist Review* 109 (1926): 839-48.
"Some Religious Aspects of the Kansas Struggle." *Journal of Religion* 7 (1927): 578-95.
"Some Salient Characteristics of Frontier Religion." *American Historical Review* 28 (1923): 431-46.
"Some Significant Factors in American Church History." *Journal of Religion* 7 (1927): 1-15.
"Stevens, Abel." *DAB* 17:604-5.
"Stuart, Charles Macaulay." *DAB* 18:163-64.
"Taylor, John." *DAB* 18:330-31.
"Thomason, Edward." *DAB* 18:482-83.

THESES BY WILLIAM WARREN SWEET

"The Activities of a Church as an Auxiliary Agent to the Government in the War of the Rebellion as Illustrated by the Methodist Episcopal Church." Ph.D. dissertation, University of Pennsylvania, 1912. [Later published as *The Methodist Episcopal Church and the Civil War*.]
"The Influence of the German Chorale upon Christian Music." B.D. thesis, Drew Theological Seminary, 1906.
"Theories of the Atonement." M.Th. thesis, Crozer Theological Seminary, 1907.

SELECTED BOOK REVIEWS BY WILLIAM WARREN SWEET

The Episcopal Church in the United States, 1800-1840, by William W. Manross. *American Historical Review* 45 (1940): 477.
History of American Congregationalism, by Gaius G. Atkins and Frederick L. Fagley. *Mississippi Valley Historical Review* 29 (1943): 629-30.
A History of Congregationalism in Nebraska, by Charles J. Kennedy. *American Historical Review* 44 (1938): 223.
A History of the Archdiocese of Boston, by Robert H. Lord. *American Historical Review* 50 (1945): 542-44.
Home Missions on the American Frontier, by Colin B. Goodykoontz. *American Historical Review* 46 (1940): 168-69.
Missions and the American Mind, by Kenneth S. Latourette. *Mississippi Valley Historical Review* 37 (1950): 114-15.
The Moravian Indian Mission on White River, edited by Lawrence H. Gipson. *Mississippi Valley Historical Review* 26 (1940): 575-76.

Religion Follows the Frontier, by Winfred E. Garrison, *Church History* 1 (1932): 58-59.

Religion in America, by Willard L. Sperry. *Christendom* 11 (1946): 516-18.

The Society of the Sacred Heart in North America, by Louise Callan. *Mississippi Valley Historical Review* 25 (1938): 410-11.

The United States and Civilization, by John U. Nef. *Mississippi Valley Historical Review* 29 (1942): 117-19.

MANUSCRIPT COLLECTIONS

Chicago. University of Chicago. Regenstein Library, Department of Special Collections. Presidents' Papers, ca. 1925-1945.

Chicago. University of Chicago. Regenstein Library, Department of Special Collections. William Warren Sweet Papers.

Dallas. Southern Methodist University. Bridwell Library. William Warren Sweet Papers.

Dallas. Southern Methodist University. Perkins School of Theology. Deans' Files (Deans Eugene B. Hawk and Merrimon Cuninggim).

Greencastle, Ind. DePauw University Archives. Presidents' Files (President George R. Grose).

Greencastle, Ind. DePauw University Archives. William Warren Sweet Collection.

Madison, N.J. Drew University. Rose Memorial Library, Methodist Historical Collection. Letters of William Warren Sweet.

NEWSPAPERS

Baldwin Criterion, Baldwin City, Kansas.
Baldwin Ledger, Baldwin City, Kansas.
Chicago Tribune, Chicago, Illinois.
Emporia [Kansas] *Weekly Gazette*, Emporia, Kansas.
Salina Daily Republican-Journal, Salina, Kansas.
Topeka Capitol, Topeka, Kansas.
Wesleyan Advance, Salina, Kansas.

UNIVERSITY PUBLICATIONS, TRANSCRIPTS, AND COLLECTIONS

Columbia University

"History, Economics and Public Law." Columbia University Bulletin of Information, 5th ser., no. 10. New York: Columbia University, 1905.

New York. Columbia University. Low Memorial Library, Columbiana Collection. History Department Classbook, 1904-1922.

DePauw University

"Alumni News Letter." DePauw University Bulletin, 3d ser., 1 (1914): 4.
"Asbury College of Liberal Arts." DePauw University Bulletin, pt. 1, 2d ser., 10 (1913).
"College of Liberal Arts Annual Catalogue 1916-1917." DePauw University Bulletin, 3d ser., 4 (1917).
Junior Class of DePauw University. *The Mirage*. Greencastle, Ind.: De-Pauw University, 1916 and 1917.

Drew University

Drew Theological Seminary, Madison, N.J. Official transcript of William Warren Sweet, 1903-1906.
TOLLEY, WILLIAM P., ed. *Alumni Record of Drew Theological Seminary.* Madison, N.J.: Drew Theological Seminary, 1926.
Year Book of Drew Theological Seminary, 1904-1905. Madison, N.J.: Drew Theological Seminary, 1905.

Kansas Wesleyan University

Annual Catalogue of the Kansas Wesleyan University for the Twelfth Academic Year, 1897-98. Salina, Kans.: Kansas Wesleyan University, 1898.
Songs of Kansas Wesleyan University. Salina, Kans.: Kansas Wesleyan University, 1909.
Wesleyan Advance, vol. 9 (1898), vol. 10 (1899).

Ohio Wesleyan University

Catalogue of Ohio Wesleyan University, no. 56. Delaware, Ohio: Ohio Wesleyan University, 1900.
Catalogue of Ohio Wesleyan University, no. 57. Delaware, Ohio: Ohio Wesleyan University, 1901.
College Transcript [student newspaper], Delaware, Ohio.
Junior Class of Ohio Wesleyan University. *The Bijou*. Columbus, Ohio: Champlin Press, 1901.
Ohio Wesleyan Transcript [student newspaper], Delaware, Ohio.
Ohio Wesleyan University, Delaware, Ohio. Official transcript of William Warren Sweet, 1898-1902.

Reports of the President and Other Officers of Ohio Wesleyan University for the College Year 1913-14. Delaware, Ohio: Ohio Wesleyan University, 1914.

University of Chicago

"The Divinity School 1916-17." *University of Chicago Circular of Information* 17 (1917): 65-67.
"The Divinity School 1921-22." *University of Chicago Circular of Information* 21 (1921): 66-70.
"The Divinity School 1925-26." *University of Chicago Announcements* 25 (1925): 58-62.
"The Divinity School 1927-28." *University of Chicago Announcements* 27 (1927): 60.

University of Pennsylvania

AMES, HERMAN V. *Proposed Amendments to the Constitution of the United States during the First Century of Its History.* American Historical Association Annual Report. Washington, D.C.: Government Printing Office, 1897.
University of Pennsylvania. Graduate School of Arts and Sciences, Philosophy Department Records. Official transcript of William Warren Sweet, 1907-1912.

OTHER BOOKS

AHLSTROM, SYDNEY E. *A Religious History of the American People.* New Haven: Yale University Press, 1972.
BACON, LEONARD W. *A History of American Christianity.* New York: Charles Scribner, 1901.
BAIRD, ROBERT. *Religion in the United States of America.* Edinburgh: Blackie & Son, 1844.
BAUGHMAN, ROBERT W. *Kansas in Maps.* Topeka: Kansas State Historical Society, 1961.
BERGER, PETER L. and LUCKMANN, THOMAS. *The Social Construction of Reality.* New York: Doubleday, 1966.
BILLINGTON, RAY A. *Frederick Jackson Turner.* San Marino, Calif.: Huntington Library, 1973.
BODO, JOHN R. *The Protestant Clergy and Public Issues, 1812-1848.* Princeton, N.J.: Princeton University Press, 1954.

BOWDEN, HENRY W. *Church History in the Age of Science.* Chapel Hill, N.C.: University of North Carolina Press, 1971.

BRAMWELL, RUBY P. *City on the Move: The Story of Salina.* Salina, Kans.: Survey Press, 1969.

CASE, SHIRLEY JACKSON. *The Christian Philosophy of History.* Chicago: University of Chicago Press, 1943.

————. *The Evolution of Early Christianity: A Genetic Study of First Century Christianity in Relation to Its Religious Environment.* Chicago: University of Chicago Press, 1914.

————. *The Social Origins of Christianity.* Chicago: University of Chicago Press, 1923.

CHASE, A. W. *Dr. Chase's Third, Last, and Complete Receipt Book and Household Physician.* Detroit: F. B. Dickerson, 1902.

CROSS, WHITNEY R. *The Burned-Over District: The Social and Intellectual History of Enthusiastic Religion in Western New York, 1800-1850.* New York: Cornell University Press, 1950.

DORCHESTER, DANIEL. *Christianity in the United States from the First Settlement Down to the Present Time.* New York: Phillips & Hunt, 1888.

EBRIGHT, HOMER K. *The History of Baker University.* Baldwin, Kans.: Baker University, 1951.

FAIRCHILD, HENRY P. *The Melting-Pot Mistake.* Boston: Little, Brown, 1926.

GARLAND, HAMLIN. *Crumbling Idols.* Chicago: Stone & Kimball, 1894.

GOODSPEED, THOMAS W. *The Story of the University of Chicago, 1890-1925.* Chicago: University of Chicago Press, 1925.

GRANT, MADISON. *The Passing of the Great Race.* New York: Charles Scribner, 1916.

GREELEY, HORACE. *An Overland Journey from New York to San Francisco.* New York: Saxton, Barker, 1860.

HANDLIN, OSCAR. *Race and Nationality in American Life.* Boston: Little, Brown, 1957.

HANDY, ROBERT T. *A Christian America.* London: Oxford University Press, 1971.

HIGHAM, JOHN. *History.* New York: Harper & Row, Harper Torchbooks, 1973.

————. *Strangers in the Land.* New Brunswick, N.J.: Rutgers University Press, 1955.

HOFSTADTER, RICHARD. *The Age of Reform.* New York: Random House, Vintage Books, 1955.

————. *The Progressive Historians: Turner, Beard, Parrington.* New York: Random House, 1968.

———— and METZGER, WALTER. *The Development of Academic Freedom in the United States.* New York: Columbia University Press, 1955.

HOLTER, DON W. *Fire on the Prairie: Methodism in the History of Kansas.* N.p.: Editorial Board of the Kansas Methodist History, 1969.

HUBBART, HENRY C. *Ohio Wesleyan's First Hundred Years.* Delaware, Ohio: Ohio Wesleyan University, 1943.

HYNES, WILLIAM J. *Shirley Jackson Case and the Chicago School.* Chico, Calif.: Scholars Press, 1981.

JENNINGS, LOUIS B. *The Bibliography and Biography of Shirley Jackson Case.* Chicago: University of Chicago Press, 1949.

MCMASTER, JOHN BACH. *A History of the People of the United States,* 8 vols. New York: Appleton, 1883-1913.

MCNEILL, JOHN T.; SPINKA, MATTHEW; and WILLOUGHBY, HAROLD R., eds. *Environmental Factors in Christian History.* Chicago: University of Chicago Press, 1939.

MANHART, GEORGE B. *DePauw through the Years,* 2 vols. Greencastle, Ind.: DePauw University, 1962.

MARTY, MARTIN E. *Righteous Empire.* New York: Dial Press, 1970.

MATHEWS, SHAILER. *The Spiritual Interpretation of History,* 2d ed. Cambridge: Harvard University Press, 1920.

MILBURN, WILLIAM H. *Lance, Cross, and Canoe.* New York: Derby & Jackson, 1857.

MODE, PETER G. *The Frontier Spirit in American Christianity.* New York: Macmillan, 1923.

————. *Source Book and Bibliographical Guide for American Church History.* Menasha, Wisc.: George Banta, 1921.

NYE, RUSSEL B. *Midwestern Progressive Politics.* New York: Harper & Row, Harper Torchbooks, 1965.

QUANDT, JEAN B. *From the Small Town to the Great Community: The Social Thought of Progressive Intellectuals.* New Brunswick, N.J.: Rutgers University Press, 1970.

REEVES, FLOYD W., ed. *The University of Chicago Survey,* 12 vols. Chicago: University of Chicago Press, 1933. Vol. 3: *The University Faculty,* chap. 4: "Scholarly Reputation."

ROBINSON, JAMES H. *The New History*. New York: Macmillan, 1912.

ROGERS, ROBERT W. *History of Babylonia and Assyria*. New York: Eaton & Mains, 1900.

ROWE, HENRY K. *The History of Religion in the United States*. New York: Macmillan, 1924.

SAVETH, EDWARD N. *American Historians and European Immigrants, 1875-1925*. New York: Russell & Russell, 1965.

SINCLAIR, ANDREW. *Prohibition: The Era of Excess*. Boston: Little, Brown, 1962.

SMITH, PAGE. *As a City Set upon a Hill: The Town in American History*. New York: Knopf, 1966.

SOLOMAN, BARBARA M. *Ancestors and Immigrants*. Chicago: University of Chicago Press, Phoenix Books, 1972.

SPERRY, WILLARD L. *Religion in America*. Cambridge: Cambridge University Press, 1946; New York: Macmillan, 1946.

STORR, RICHARD J. *Harper's University*. Chicago: University of Chicago Press, 1966.

TAYLOR, GEORGE R., ed. *The Turner Thesis*. Boston: Heath, 1956.

TIMBERLAKE, JAMES H. *Prohibition and the Progressive Movement*. Cambridge: Harvard University Press, 1966.

TURNER, FREDERICK J. *The Frontier in American History*. New York: Henry Holt, 1920.

VANDERHOOF, JACK W. *The Time Now Past: Kansas Wesleyan University, 1886-1961*. Salina, Kans.: Kansas Wesleyan University, 1962.

VEYSEY, LAURENCE R. *The Emergence of the American University*. Chicago: University of Chicago Press, 1965.

WISH, HARVEY. *The American Historian*. London and New York: Oxford University Press, 1960.

ZORNOW, WILLIAM F. *Kansas: A History of the Jayhawk State*. Norman, Okla.: University of Oklahoma Press, 1957.

OTHER ARTICLES AND RECORDS

BALDWIN, SIMEON E. "Religion Still the Key to History." *American Historical Review* 12 (1907): 219-43.

BAYLES, GEORGE J. "American Ecclesiology." In *Annual Report of the American Historical Association for the Year 1900*. Washington, D.C.: Government Printing Office (1901): 129-38.

BEARD, CHARLES A. "Written History as an Act of Faith." *American Historical Review* 39 (1934): 219-31.

BOWDEN, HENRY W. "Modern Developments in the Interpretation of Church History." *Historical Magazine of the Protestant Episcopal Church* 43 (1974): 105-23.

BRAUER, JERALD C. "Changing Perspectives on Religion in America." In *Reinterpretation in American Church History*, edited by Jerald C. Brauer. Chicago: University of Chicago Press, 1968.

CASE, SHIRLEY JACKSON. "The Historical Study of Religion." *Journal of Religion* 1 (1921): 1-17.

CHRISTIE, FRANCIS A. "Report of the Conference on the Teaching of Church History." In *Annual Report of the American Historical Association for the Year 1904*. Washington, D.C.: Government Printing Office (1905): 216-18.

CLEBSCH, WILLIAM A. "A New Historiography of American Religion." *Historical Magazine of the Protestant Episcopal Church* 32 (1963): 225-57.

GAUSTAD, EDWIN S. "Religion in America: History and Historiography." *American Historical Association Pamphlet*, no. 260. Washington, D.C.: American Historical Association, 1973.

HOFSTADTER, RICHARD. "Turner and the Frontier Myth." *American Scholar* 18 (1949): 94-111.

HUTCHINSON, WILLIAM T. "John Bach McMaster." In *The Marcus W. Jernegan Essays in American Historiography*, edited by William T. Hutchinson. Chicago: University of Chicago Press, 1937.

JAMESON, J. FRANKLIN. "The American Acta Sanctorum." *American Historical Review* (1908): 286-302.

Journal of the Uniting Conference of the Methodist Church. New York: Methodist Publishing House, 1939.

Kansas. *State Census of 1885*, vol. 79.

McLAUGHLIN, ANDREW C. "American History and American Democracy." *American Historical Review* 10 (1915): 256-70.

McNEILL, HAROLD. "William Warren Sweet." Typewritten. An essay based on an interview with William Warren Sweet, Jr., on November 10, 1971, in Fort Worth, Texas.

MARTY, MARTIN E. "The American Mainstream: Generalizations about the Protestant Denominations in the General Histories of American Christianity." Typewritten. Chicago, 1956.

MAY, HENRY F. "The Recovery of American Religious History." *American Historical Review* 70 (1964-1965): 79-92.

MEAD, SIDNEY E. "Professor Sweet's Religion and Culture in America." *Church History* 22 (1953): 33-49.

Mississippi Valley Historical Association. "Minutes of the Twenty-seventh Annual Meeting" (Spring 1934). *Mississippi Valley Historical Review* 21 (1934): 213-14.

PELIKAN, JAROSLAV. "Methodism's Contribution to America." In *The History of American Methodism*, edited by Emory S. Bucke. New York: Abingdon Press, 1964.

RANDALL, J. H., JR., and HAINES, G., IV. "Controlling Assumptions in the Practice of American Historians." In *Theory and Practices in Historical Study: A Report of the Committee on Historiography*. New York: Social Science Research Council Bulletin no. 54, 1946, pp. 97-145.

ROBINSON, JAMES H. "Sacred and Profane History." In *Annual Report of the American Historical Association for the Year 1899*. Washington, D.C.: Government Printing Office, 1900, 1:528-40.

U.S. Department of the Interior Census Office. *Compendium of the Eleventh Census*, 1890, vol. 1: *Population*.

OTHER THESES

JONES, ARCHIE H. "American Protestantism and the Science of History." Ph.D. dissertation, University of Chicago, 1954.

LINDSAY, JONATHAN A. "A Critical Evaluation of William Warren Sweet as a Writer of American Church History." Th.D. dissertation, Southern Baptist Theological Seminary, 1967.

MODE, PETER G. "The Influence of the Black Death on the English Monasteries." Ph.D. dissertation, University of Chicago, 1916.

RILEY, WILLIAM F. "The Influence of Turner's Frontier Thesis upon American Religious Historiography." M.A. thesis, Western Kentucky University, 1974.

WURSTER, STEPHEN. "The Modernism of Shailer Mathews: A Study in American Religious Progressivism." Ph.D. dissertation, University of Iowa, 1972.

SELECTED REVIEWS OF BOOKS BY WILLIAM WARREN SWEET

BILLINGTON, RAY A. Review of *The American Churches. American Historical Review* 54 (1949): 438-39.

COX, ISAAC J. Review of *A History of Latin America. Mississippi Valley Historical Review* 6 (1919): 435.

ESAREY, LOGAN. Review of *Circuit-Rider Days in Indiana*. *Mississippi Valley Historical Review* 3 (1916): 250.

FISH, C. R. Review of *The Methodist Episcopal Church and the Civil War*. *American Historical Review* 18 (1913): 405-6.

FLETCHER, ROBERT S. Review of *Religion on the American Frontier*, vol. 3: *The Congregationalists*. *Mississippi Valley Historical Review* 26 (1940): 570.

GARRISON, WINFRED E. Review of *The Story of Religions in America*. *Christian Century* 47 (1930): 1627.

GEWEHR, W. M. Review of *The Story of Religions in America*. *American Historical Review* 37 (1932): 349-50.

LATOURETTE, KENNETH S. Review of *The American Churches*. *Mississippi Valley Historical Review* 35 (1948): 535-36.

MORSE, JARVIS M. Review of *Men of Zeal*. *Mississippi Valley Historical Review* 22 (1936): 569-70.

NETTELS, CURTIS. Review of *Religion in Colonial America*. *Mississippi Valley Historical Review* 29 (1942): 441.

SMITH, H. SHELTON. Review of *Religion in the Development of American Culture*. *Theology Today* 10 (1954): 563-65.

STEARNS, RAYMOND P. Review of *Religion in Colonial America*. *American Historical Review* 49 (1944): 490-91.

SWANEY, C. B. Review of *Circuit-Rider Days along the Ohio*. *Mississippi Valley Historical Review* 10 (1923): 339.

WISH, HARVEY. Review of *Religion in the Development of American Culture*. *American Historical Review* 59 (1953): 138-40.

OBITUARIES AND BIOGRAPHICAL SKETCHES

American Historical Review 64 (1959): 831.

"Father of American Church History Dies." *Christian Century* 76 (1959): 71.

IRWIN, WILLIAM A. "William Warren Sweet." Funeral eulogy. Typewritten. Dallas, 1959.

Mississippi Valley Historical Review 46 (1959): 180-81.

New York Times, January 5, 1959.

SWEET, PAUL W. "Biographical Introduction." In *A History of Methodism in Northwest Kansas*, by William H. Sweet. Salina, Kans.: Kansas Wesleyan University, 1920.

Who Was Who in America, 1951-1960. Chicago: A. N. Marquis, 1963.

Index

161